HIDDEN TREASURE

The Riches of the Eucharist

Louis Kaczmarek

M. B. S.
PO Box 1701, Plattsburgh, NY 12901
Phone (518) 561-8193 Fax (518) 566-7103
ACFP2000@aol.com www.ACFP2000.com

ISBN 0-937495-38-7

Dedication

To Mary,
the World's First Love
who gave us Jesus,
the World's Greatest Love.

TABLE OF CONTENTS

Foreword

"The Holy Eucharist contains the entire spiritual treasure of the Church, that is, Christ Himself, our Passover and Living Bread." So has spoken Pope John Paul II, the 265th successor to St. Peter.

In *Hidden Treasure,* Louis Kaczmarek sets about the task of asking a simple question: "Where can we find God?" The pages of his excellent volume provide the astounding answer: the pearl of great price, the hidden treasure, is Christ as He reveals Himself in the great sacrifice and sacrament of the Holy Eucharist. We find God in the Christ of the Eucharist, the "entire spiritual treasure of the Church."

Today more than ever, people are looking for visible signs of commitment, love, trust, faith and devotion. No more visible sign could we have than the sign God has given us in the Holy Eucharist: in bread broken and wine poured out as sacrament and sacrifice.

In this magnificent spiritual treatise on the Holy Eucharist, the author includes the testimony of the ages to support the Church's doctrine of the Real Presence, as well as to foster an appreciation of the Eucharist as a source of unity and bond of love within the Church.

Such strong testimony includes Sacred Scripture, the writings of the Fathers of the Church, the witness of countless saints whose dedicated Christian lives flowed from their great love for and devotion to Christ in the Blessed Sacrament, and the Statements of the Church's Magisterium.

In an age of unbelief and so much self-seeking, in a world of distractions, confusion, tumult, and indifference to the Church and her doctrines, the pages of this book call all Catholics to renew and rededicate themselves to a greater love, devotion and appreciation for Christ's gift of the Eucharist. In particular, the reader is challenged to observe the devotional practice of prayer before the Blessed Sacrament, as well to receive Communion frequently and worthily.

Every celebration of the Eucharist and reception of Holy Communion is a visible statement of our re-commitment in faith and love to our belief in the Real Presence of Christ in the Eucharist. Every visit with Christ in the Blessed Sacrament provides the unique opportunity for the beloved and the lover to speak to each other heart to heart.

These key moments in the Catholic religious experience can only help to reinforce the teachings of the Church that "sacramental communion received during Mass is the most perfect participation in the eucharistic celebration...Both private and public devotion toward the Eucharist,...including devotion outside Mass, are strongly encouraged" *(Holy Communion and Worship of the Eucharist Outside Mass,* Sacred Congregation for Divine Worship, #13 and 19).

May this thought-provoking and inspirational treatment of the Holy Eucharist inspire us to respond to the question, "Where can we find God?" with the faith-filled and loving question addressed to Jesus by the "Rock" on whom He built His Church: "Lord, to whom shall we go? You have the words of everlasting life" (John 6:68).

Most Rev. Edward M. Grosz, D.D., V.G.
Auxiliary Bishop of Buffalo

Introduction

Intimations of Divinity

The mute testimony of the cemetery speaks louder than the voice of any herald, or the greatest oracle. No sermon has ever had a more profound, piercing, lasting effect. "Is this it?" "Is this all there is to life?" Are our hearts merely "muffled drums beating a death march to the grave?"

Without a Supreme Being in our lives, there is no inspiring goal for us other than self interest. There is no room for tenderness, generosity, helpfulness. Marriage becomes a matter of biology, not fidelity. Society offers us few successful role models to pattern a life destined for a future world, but rather furnishes us with many diversions to distract us from the effort.

Even among the wildest, most remote pagans in the world, there is found the worship of some deity whom they recognize as supreme, on whom man depends. You can find savage people without laws but never without some god that they worship with prayer and sacrifice. Long ago, the pagan Cicero said: "When we contemplate the heavens, we arrive at the conviction that they are all guided by a Being of surpassing skill."

The harmony of the universe, the mystery of creation, the incredible design of our bodies, absolutely demand a planning intelligence, and speak of a Creator telling us we are here for a purpose, that we have a job to do, a destiny to fulfill.

The haunting blast of a ship's horn at sea, the eerie calling of a train's shrill whistle in the distance, the chilling peal of a church bell, are all soul-stirring tugs at our heart strings, like a premonition, summoning us to the call of another land, another world.

New Life in a New Place

He who created the sky before He fashioned the bird, who made the water before He formed the fish, must have created a place of abode to answer the yearnings of my heart. It is this of which St. Paul speaks when he says, "No eye has seen, nor ear heard, nor the heart of man conceived what God has prepared for those who love Him."

The closing of the casket does not terminate our life any more than an airplane departure terminal ends our journey. The casket merely closes the door to a world that has limitations and opens up to another that has no boundaries—just as the airplane lifts one from the restrictions of earth to unfathomable space.

The first words of the Creed are: "I believe in God." And doesn't our heart constantly cry out "God! God! God!" with each pulsating beat in search of the intelligence who fashioned it, for "the tongue reveals what the heart contains"; and instinctively, a person in danger, shock or crisis, will cry out: "Oh my God!"

St. Augustine: Man's Restless Heart

St. Augustine's words, "Thou has made us for Thyself, and our hearts are restless, until they rest in Thee" were but an echo of King Solomon's, "Vanity of vanities, and all is vanity" except to love God.

There is only one problem, then, on which all my existence, my peace, and my happiness depend: to discover God. And when I seek God I seek nothing that can perish in a grave. "I seek not corporal grace," as St. Augustine says,

> nor transient beauty, nor splendor, nor melodious sounds, nor sweet fragrance of flowers, nor odorous essence, nor honeyed manna, nor grace of form, nor anything pleasing to the flesh. None of these things do I seek when I seek my God. But I seek a light exceeding all light, which the eyes cannot see; a voice sweeter than all sound, which the ear cannot hear; a sweetness above all sweetness, which the tongue cannot

taste; a fragrance about all fragrance, which the senses cannot perceive; a mysterious and divine embrace, which the body cannot feel. For this light shines without radiance, this voice is heard without striking the air, this fragrance is perceived though the wind does not bear it, this taste inebriates with no palate to relish it, and this embrace is felt in the center of the soul.

The Catholic Church

The great question, then, is: where can we find God whom we all hunger for? We need but direct our footsteps to the door of the Catholic Church and "enter this door as if the floor within were gold; and every wall of jewels all of wealth untold; as if a choir in robes of fire were singing here; nor shout nor rush but hush...for God is here!*

---

*This profound quotation, from an unidentified source, appeared on a holy card in the 1950's.

1.

Too Good Not to Be True

The Eternal Present of God

God, dwelling in the tabernacle, is the God of the eternal present. Like a vast panorama, the past, present and future are all spread out before Him. He sees them all, as it were, in one view. Strictly speaking, there is no past or future to God. To show that He lives in the eternal present, He said to Moses: "I am Who I am."

His words too are in the eternal present: "The kingdom of heaven is like a treasure hidden in a field; he who finds it hides it and in his joy goes and sells all that he has and buys that field" (Matt. 13:44), and "The kingdom of heaven is like a merchant in search of fine pearls. When he finds a single pearl of great price, he goes and sells all that he has and buys it" (Matt. 13:45).

Christ is that "treasure," that "pearl," and the sanctuary lamp in every Catholic

Church is the beacon light flickering this truth, so secret, so public, so mysterious, so simple.

To win people, to raise them to share in His life, to be able to converse with them, God came to earth as a child in Bethlehem and remains with us in the Eucharist.

In our moments of yearning, our hearts hunger for God. Sometimes we catch a glimpse of eternity in a moment of time; a hint of another richer, fuller life. Hence would Edna St. Vincent Millay write; "I came upon no wine so wonderful as thirst."

Charles de Foucald

One who thirsted eagerly for God was Charles de Foucald whose prodigal and shocking way of life provoked so much gossip in Paris that he was the butt of violent feelings and jokes among French soldiers.

Born September 15, 1858, of fabulous wealth, at one point of his shady life he stated: "I was so completely selfish, so completely vain, so completely irreligious, and utterly given over to wickedness, that I was only one step away from insanity."

God seemed to him to be infinitely remote—if He existed at all! He used to enter St. Augustine Church in Paris, repeating over and over "My God, if You exist, let me come to know You." One day, as a priest elevated the Consecrated Host, he was overheard to say: "My God, You are real!"

"In a single instant," he said, "my heart was touched and I believed." The Eucharist, until his death, dominated his whole life. To stir others to seek and find God dwelling in the tabernacle that they too may be touched to the quick, share in his discovery, and come home to the Creator, "that Power which erring women call chance," he composed this prayer:

> Oh Jesus present in the Blessed Sacrament in our churches, You give us solace and refuge; You give us faith, hope, love and hospitality. You build for us an inner retreat, an ardent repose. Help us to seek You and find You in the tabernacle.

What can be more exciting, inspiring, engage one's attention more, and crystallize one's own belief, than Protestants who have found Him in the tabernacle.

Elizabeth Ann Seton

Elizabeth Ann Seton, a convert, was the first native-born United States citizen to be canonized. What brought her into the faith, and what seemed to her too good to be true, was the Real Presence of our Lord in the Blessed Sacrament.

Upon the death of her husband, she was seeking peace of mind in St. Paul's Episcopal Church in New York. She later wrote to a friend: "I got in a side pew in which I was positioned in such a way that I was facing St. Peter's Catholic Church in the next street. And I found myself speaking to the Blessed Sacrament in the Catholic Church, instead of looking at the naked altar where I was...."

The Convert Leslie E. Dunkin

A former Protestant minister, Leslie E. Dunkin, wrote these thought provoking words in a letter to his minister friends:

> The contrast between any non-Catholic or Protestant church and any Catholic Church has helped convince me concerning the Divine Presence. Any Protestant building requires the presence of people, and they in the right mood, to feel even the presence of Christ's spirit. Any Catholic Church with its burning tabernacle light possesses for all—both Catholic and non-Catholic—a feeling of hushed silence. The Catholic knows this to be the Divine Presence in His tabernacle. After having attended Catholic Mass with a reasonable understanding of its meaning, I found that any non-Catholic church service at its best lacks what is always experienced at Catholic Mass or even alone in a Catholic Church—the immediate Divine Presence and the keen sense of this presence.

Robert Browning and Other Converts

Robert Browning, the famous English poet, and a non-Catholic, attended a Mass during a tour of Italy. He was so inspired by the ceremony and the sacredness of the atmosphere, that he clutched the arm of his companion and exclaimed: "My God! This is too good not to be true."

Erick Sokolsky, son of the famous columnist George Sokolsky, writing of his conversion from Judaism to Catholicism, declared: "I used to go to Mass at St. Patrick's Cathedral. I had no idea of what the church taught. I knew only that its ritual was warm, majestic, powerful. Going to Mass at St. Patrick's became a thrilling experience for me. For the first time, I felt that I was in the presence of God."

Conversion of Elsie Briggs

Elsie Briggs submitted this story of her conversion to the *Boston Pilot:*

> There is nothing brilliant or scholarly that attracted me to the Roman Catholic Church. What attracted me to Catholicism was love.
>
> It all goes back about ten years when beaten and disillusioned I crept into the rear of the Mission Church in Roxbury to rest. I didn't go in because I was attracted to the church, or because I sought spiritual refreshment; it was only a place to sit down and get off my feet and find, if possible, a few moments of forgetfulness.
>
> How long I sat there, I don't know, but I suddenly became aware of something living. There was an actual presence all around that seemed to emanate from

the altar. It was pleasing and restful to feel. And without half realizing what I was doing I moved up front until I was sitting in the first pew.

The weariness and strain all fell away and a great sense of peace and love came over me, combined with an intense desire to sleep...

And right here and now I want to explain that at that time I knew absolutely nothing about the Catholic teachings. No one had ever told me of the Host or of the ever-present living God on the altar....

For the first time I learned how wrong the average Protestant is in his supposed knowledge of the Catholic Faith. There certainly is nothing more ignorant than nine Protestants out of ten, when it comes to the teachings of the Church of Rome.

All the old wives' tales, all the lies I had heard from childhood about Catholics were exposed by the light of truth. What a pity there should be such ignorance of God's truth and how many Protestants, such as I was then, would gladly and eagerly accept the church and her teachings if they only knew the truth that sets one free....

The saints were fully aware that Christ in the Blessed Sacrament is a reality—that in the Blessed Sacrament His heart is living, beating, waiting to refresh us with His graces.

St. Dominic Savio and Fr. Balthasar Alvarez, S.J.

One who felt his heart beating in union with the Sacred Heart in the tabernacle was St. Dominic Savio. Only fifteen years of age when he died, kneeling six hours a day before the Blessed Sacrament was not sufficient for him. His extraordinary devotion to the Blessed Sacrament merited him the title: "Child of the Holy Eucharist."

The holy Jesuit, Fr. Balthasar Alvarez, often would direct his eyes towards the place he knew the Blessed Sacrament was. Whenever possible, he spent the entire night before it. He used to weep when he saw the palaces of the great ones of this world filled with people and the churches so abandoned, when they had the supreme Sovereign of the world within.

St. John Francis Regis & St. Dominic

St. John Francis Regis was often heard to say: "What in the world can engage my heart beside Thee, my Lord?" He was observed frequently in prayer before the Blessed Sacrament, like a seraphim, motionless for many hours. In the village of St. Bonnet le Froid, he was seen kneeling, the entire night, outside of the locked doors of the church adoring his God.

Every night, after his friars had gone to bed, St. Dominic would go to the church, and there, near the Lord, spend the long exacting hours of the night in prayer where he found interior consolation, solace, secret joys, ineffable delights, which our Lord poured out from His enchanting Heart in this holy Sacrament of love. When exhausted nature at last forced him to take some repose, he would lie on the stone floor of the sanctuary for a few hours sleep, never wanting to leave his Lord.

St. Francis Xavier and Leon Dupont

St. Francis Xavier would rest from his apostolic labors before the tabernacle spending entire nights upon the altar steps telling the Savior of his suffering and asking Him for comfort and strength.

Leon Dupont spent much time in encouraging people to make nightly adoration before the Blessed Sacrament. In two months time he convinced seventy-four men to do so. It was an inspiring sight to see men of all walks of life—laborers, students, merchants, military, and state officials—coming to perform their nightly adoration.

St. Nicholas Van Flue

Spending long hours before the tabernacle, nocturnally, was the reason patriots, politicians, historians and poets of all creeds have sung the praises of St. Nicholas Van Flue, to such an extent that is may be safely asserted that no religious figure in the history of Switzerland has given rise to so varied and voluminous a body of literature.

The oldest of his ten children, a son, states:

> My father always retired to rest at the same time as his children and servants; but every night I saw him get up again, and heard him praying in his room until morning. Often he would go in the silence of the night to the old church of St. Nicholas or to other holy places.

Bishop Fulton Sheen

While Bishop Fulton J. Sheen was a young priest staying in London, it was his duty to open and close the doors of the church every day. He saw the same man, upon opening the doors for morning Mass, that he had seen the night before when he locked the doors. The man made a practice of nocturnal adoration before the Blessed Sacrament without fail.

While in the Holy Land in 1925 making a pilgrimage, a priest was traveling through Smyrna, Turkey. It was shortly after the Turks had pillaged and burned the Christian section of the city. Approaching a convent, he saw a nun who was from Ireland and asked, "Don't you feel lost in this out-of-the-way corner of the world, so far from your home in Ireland?"

Pointing to the tabernacle, she replied: "Father, wherever the Blessed Sacrament is, there I am at home. For there is my Lord and my God."

Her contemporary and countryman, Matt Talbot, echoed her words often, saying: "How can anyone be lonely with our Lord in the Blessed Sacrament?"

From Pope to layman, intellectual to unlettered, king to peasant, saint to sinner, for two thousand years, people in every country of the world have found healing, comfort, enlightenment and strength, and have had the flame of love rekindled, in the presence of the Blessed Sacrament.

Blessed Margaret of Castello

From the Eucharistic throne, streams of light and power, joy and peace, comfort and blessings pour into countless human hearts that come to Him with confidence, humility and love. An outstanding case is that of Blessed Margaret of Castello who was born a hunchback, midget, blind, lame and ugly, and was an embarrassment to her proud, wealthy and powerful thirteenth-century parents, who had her walled-up beside a chapel at the age of six. She could not get out, but could attend Mass and receive Holy Communion through a small opening cut into the wall of the church. On the other side of the cell was another opening through which food was passed to her.

With tear-stained face, the dark lowering clouds of despair come swirling in upon her soul leaving her sick at heart and bewildered. Never again could she play with children, as her father wished her to die hidden from the world and his rejection.

She struggled to do the only thing left to her—pray. For thirteen years her only companions were the Blessed Sacrament and silence. She would tell the priest who gave her Holy Communion, after struggling against complete hopelessness and discouragement: "Father, I am not good enough to be so near to God."

Even though we cannot see Him, spending time in the shadow of the tabernacle, so near to our Lord, we grow spiritually warmed by the rays of His invisible graces like a plant absorbing sunlight. You cannot see the plant grow, but you can see that it has grown; in like manner you cannot see your soul progressing spiritually yet experience proves it does. Our Lord said: "Blessed are they who do not see and believe."

King John Sobieski and Pope Innocent XI

It was the firm belief of Christ in the Blessed Sacrament that made King John Sobieski of Poland the great monarch that he was. He had been trained by his parents to always have recourse to our Lord in the Blessed Sacrament in times of trial, and to always rise to the occasion with the heart of a lion.

When asked by Pope Innocent XI to come to the aid of Catholic Europe, he gladly accepted the challenge. His great act, and the gallant rescue of Vienna in 1683 by his Polish army, was called by historians, "The last noble reflex of the great crusading impulse of the middle ages." The king made it a point to take his army of 72,000 from Cracow directly to Czestochowa, the national shrine in Poland in honor of the Blessed Virgin Mary, and requested all of his soldiers to hear Mass and receive Holy Communion before leaving for the battlefields of Vienna.

Saint Louis IX In the person of St. Louis IX were the qualities which form a great king, a hero of romance, and a saint! With his death, the century of knights ended. One day a messenger, breathless with haste, burst in upon the king with surprising and exciting news. "Your majesty," he cried, "hasten to the Church! A great miracle is occurring there. A priest is saying holy Mass, and after the consecration, instead of the host there is visible on the altar Jesus Himself in His human figure. Everybody is marveling at it. Hurry before it disappears."

To the astonishment of the messenger, the saintly monarch calmly replied:

> Let them go to see the miracle who have any doubt regarding the Real Presence of our Lord in the Holy Sacrament. As for me, even if I saw Jesus on the altar in His visible form, and touched Him with my hand, and heard His voice, I should not be more convinced than I now am,

> that He is present in the consecrated Host. The word of Christ is sufficient for me. I need no miracle.

Saint Casimir

It is said of St. Casimir, the young prince of the royal house of Poland, "His life is spent more in church than in the royal palace."

Twenty-three years of age when he died on March 4, 1484, he led a vigorous and rigorous life for God which was inspired by his pious and wise mother, his first teacher, who would not allow him to be spoiled by pomp and luxury, and always maintained a strict discipline over him.

His piety grew and developed into a great love of God. His regard for the Eucharist impressed everyone. After daily Mass, he would remain in church for two hours.

He loved to visit churches, and if the door was locked, he would kneel at the door adoring God in the tabernacle, strictly ordering his attendants to tell no one.

After his death, his holy life attracted thousands to his tomb and the faith the people had in his intercessory power with God won for them the favors they sought. So many miracles were granted that a bell in Kraziani was inscribed with the words: "Casimir, wonderful on earth, more wonderful in heaven."

When we contemplate the indescribable beauty of all the wonders of nature, when we think of all the priceless treasures in the museums and galleries, all of these works that compel the astonished admiration of men are as nothing when compared with God's Presence in the Eucharist.

Saint Wenceslaus and St. Vincent Gerosa

Thoughts of this nature led St. Wenceslaus, King of Bohemia, with his own hands, to make the altar-bread which was to be used for the Mass and would become the Blessed Sacrament, without any regard to the royal dignity he held. He who was born to wield the scepter even directed the plowing and cultivating of the field, the sowing of the seed, and the reaping of the harvest. Then he ground the grain, separated the finer flour for the oven, and made the breads which should afterward be consecrated; and these he presented, with the lowliest reverence, to the priests, to be converted into the divine Body of Jesus.

St. Vincentia Gerosa would take care of grapevines that supplied wine for Holy Mass. She cultivated and pruned them with her own hands, finding it a tremendous honor and privilege because these clusters that she had grown would become the Blood of Christ.

Personal Contact with Our Lord

We cannot prize the most Blessed Sacrament sufficiently, for it is the heart of the Church, the center of our religion, the well-spring of our Faith. Our Lord offers a fathomless depth of riches for those who will come to Him asking for His help. How interesting, how exciting, that all of the people Christ cured in the Bible, except two, were people who had made personal contact with Him! He Who waits in the tabernacle, for us to come to Him, is the the same Lord that the two blind men of Jericho cried out to: "Lord, that our eyes be opened." And Jesus, moved with compassion, touched their eyes and at once they received their sight.

He is the same Lord to whom the leper pitifully cried out: "Lord, if Thou wilt, Thou can make me clean." Stretching forth His hand, Jesus touched him and said, "I will; be thou made clean."

He is the same Lord who felt compassion for the paralytic and said to him, "Arise, take up thy pallet and go to thy house" after He had said "Thy sins are forgiven thee."

The Love of Christ and Our Response in Love

He is the same Lord who said: "I have loved you with an everlasting love" (Jer. 31:3). "See, O man, how I have been the first to love you. You were not yet in the world, the world itself did not exist, but even then I loved you. As long as I have been God I have loved you."

How He showed His love to the woman caught in adultery, saying to her accusers: "Let him who is without sin among you be the first to cast a stone at her." Turning to her, He said, "Woman, where are they? Has no one condemned thee?" "No one, Lord." And Jesus said to her "Neither will I condemn thee."

He is the same Lord that asked Peter three times, do you love Me? And Peter's three acts of love to his God were the total payment required of him for his denial—three simple acts of love! Little wonder St. Peter would say: "An act of love covers a multitude of sins!"

2.

Talisman of Highest Sanctity

Professor Contardi Ferrini

Called "The Prince of Scholars," Professor Contardo Ferrini taught law at the University of Pavia. Neither honors, nor flatteries, nor the opposition of unbelievers could in the least diminish his religious spirit. Every day he went to daily Mass and Holy Communion, then spent an hour in the evening in the presence of the Blessed Sacrament.

Modern unbelief, so widespread in higher schools of learning, could not touch him. There was no doubt or wavering for him. It is remarkable that this great scholar considered pride the greatest hindrance to the knowledge of truth. Hence, he could never insist enough on humility as the only way to the knowledge of God.

Words of holy wisdom flowed from Professor Ferrini who preferred to spend all of his spare time before Jesus in the Blessed Sacrament, saying:

> Because of the consoling effect of prayer, I waste no time in theaters, cafés, and the one thousand useless pastimes of an ill-regulated life... Life without prayer is to me inconceivable. Such a life must be like a dark night, disheartening and saddening, on which rests the curse of God, which gives no strength to withstand temptations and in which all joy of spirit is wanting. It is a puzzle to me how anyone can live such a life.

The saints knew these truths and developed an eye that could see, an ear that could hear, and a heart that conceived the indescribable greatness, worth and beauty of our Lord's Presence in the Blessed Sacrament. They asked for a great spirit of faith that they might understand better the tremendous value of our Lord's gift to us.

Students of Divine Love

While in the presence of the Blessed Sacrament they considered themselves but students in the school of divine love with Jesus as their teacher. Like St. Paul, they considered all things but loss, and counted them as nothing that they may gain Christ, which was the knowledge he spoke of that "surpasses all the knowledge." In Christ alone they found wisdom and sanctification, for Christ appeared among men, conversing with them, and showing them by His human life how God lives among men, in order that we may know how we are to live to be pleasing to God.

The saints constantly kept their gaze on the divine rays of Christ. Only too well they realized the measure of their perfection was determined by the degree of their imitation of Him. Apart from Him, all light would be darkness.

These delightful audiences with Jesus were an invaluable means of maintaining a perpetual union with Him, and often caused them to break out in transports of joy.

Herman Cohen Becomes Augustine Maria of the Blessed Sacrament

Herman Cohen, who died in Spain in 1817, was a Jewish convert who became a discalced Carmelite and took the name of Augustine Maria of the Blessed Sacrament. He was once asked: "Are you happy?" "Happy!" he exclaimed with a radiant countenance,

> I traveled over the whole earth in order to become so, but found it yields no happiness. In nature and in the theater, at splendid banquets and in the most distinguished company, everywhere have I sought happiness; where have I not sought it?—yet all in vain. But now I possess it. Yes, I am happy, perfectly happy; and do you wish to know where I find true happiness? At the feet of Jesus in the Blessed Sacrament.

St. Gerard Majella

Fr. Tannoia, who wrote the life of St. Gerard Majella, tells us one day he saw him praying before the tabernacle. Suddenly he cried out, "Lord, let me go, I pray Thee! I have work that I must do!" In his short life of only 29 years, he became the most famous wonder-worker of the eighteenth century. His mother testified after his death, "My child's only happiness was in church on his knees before the Blessed Sacrament. He would stay there till he forgot it was dinner time. He was born for heaven."

St. Rose of Lima and St. Philip Neri

St. Rose of Lima was so ardent in her love of God in the Blessed Sacrament that when she knelt in His presence the fire which sparkled in her eyes showed the flame which consumed her soul. At times she appeared like an angel. If anyone asked her what effects the Blessed Sacrament produced in her, she stammered and said she had no words to express them, but that she seemed to pass entirely into God, and was inundated with such happiness that nothing in common life could be compared to it.

St. Philip Neri had prayed so fervently before the Blessed Sacrament for the gifts of the Holy Spirit that he was filled with so much divine love and happiness that he rolled upon the floor exclaiming "Enough, enough, Lord. I can bear no more!"

Countenances which Reflect God's Light

While some experienced transports of joy, others were seen with a glow about their body. We read in Holy Scripture that Moses once conversed with God on a mountain, and afterwards, when he came down to the Jews, his countenance was so radiant with light that they were unable to look at him. Though many saints were blessed in this way, not all biographers make mention of it.

St. Ignatius Loyola

St. Ignatius Loyola, founder of the Jesuit Order, took an hour to celebrate the Holy Sacrifice of the Mass. After Mass he spent two hours in private prayer, during which time no one was admitted to speak to him except on some pressing necessity. Fr. Lewis Gonzales, who for some time governed the college under him, says,

> As often as I went to him at that time, which necessity frequently obliged me to do, I always saw his face shining with an air so bright and heavenly that, quite forgetting myself, I stood astonished in contemplating him. Nor was his countenance like that of many devout men in whom I have admired a wonderful serenity at their prayers, but it breathed something quite unusual and, as it were, divine.

Isabel Rosella, John Pascal, and other persons testified that they had sometimes beheld his countenance at prayer sparkling with radiant beams of light, and heard him say, "Oh my God! Oh my Lord! Oh that men knew Thee!"

St. Joseph Benedict LaBré and St. Paschal Baylon

Known as "The Beggar Saint of Rome," St. Joseph Benedict LaBré spent his nights sleeping in the open arches of the Colosseum and his days praying in churches. While in the presence of the Blessed Sacrament, he would have a luminous glow on his face revealing the intense fire of love for the Blessed Sacrament. Spending five to six hours at a time before the tabernacle, his face, normally colorless, glowed with a rosy hue all the while.

St. Paschal Baylon was proclaimed by the church as the patron saint of all Eucharistic Congresses and confraternities of the Blessed Sacrament. He knelt for long periods of time absorbed in prayer, his eyes fixed upon the tabernacle. The incredibly long periods which he spent before the tabernacle, kneeling without support, his clasped hands held up in front of his face, his body emitting a soft glow, had left a deep impression upon everyone who saw him. For them he was "The saint of the Blessed Sacrament."

St. Colette and St. Mary Magdalen de Pazzi

Upon receiving Holy Communion, St. Colette, a fifteenth century Poor Clare nun of France, would be rapt in ecsasy which lasted five hours. Her countenance shone with celestial brightness. She would say with incredible conviction, "My eyes, I have filled with Jesus upon whom I have fixed them at the elevation of the Host at Holy Mass and I do not wish to replace Him with any other image."

A glow was observed about St. Mary Magdalen de Pazzi, who was known for her deep love for the Blessed Sacrament, which often sent her into ecstasies. She said: "Oh Lord, You are as truly present under the sacramental species as You are in Heaven at the right hand of the Father. Because I have and possess this great wonder, I do not long for, want, or desire any other." For her, being in the presence of the Eucharistic King was a foretaste of heaven. For her, Christ was not two thousand years away in a distant heaven that cannot be spanned. He was present in the nearest tabernacle.

St. Peter of Alcantara, St. John of the Cross, and Father Louis la Nusa

When St. Peter of Alcantara was still a youth, he remained unusually long in church after attending Mass. When midday passed and he had not returned home, his mother sent a servant to search for him. The saint was found kneeling in church, his face glowing with celestial brightness.

St. John of the Cross was often seen rapt in ecstasy radiating light as he knelt in the presence of the Blessed Sacrament.

Like Peter, James and John who saw our Lord in His transfigured glory on the mountain and never wanted to leave, so too was this the experience of many saints while in the presence of the Blessed Sacrament.

Fr. Louis la Nusa, a great missionary of Sicily, was so much attached to Jesus Christ even as a young student that it seemed as if he could hardly tear himself from the presence of his beloved Lord, on account of the great delight he found there. He was commanded by his director not to remain before the Blessed Sacrament longer than an hour at a time, and when that period had elapsed it was as great a violence to him to separate from the bosom of Jesus, as for an infant to tear itself from its mother's breast. The writer of his life says, that, when he was forced to leave the church, he would stand looking at the altar and turning, again and again, as if he could not take leave of his Lord, whose presence was so sweet and so consoling.

St. Aloysius

Having spent too much time before the Blessed Sacrament, St. Aloysius too was forbidden to remain as long as he desired. He used to pass by the Blessed Sacrament, finding himself powerfully drawn, so to speak, by the sweet attractions of his Lord, and almost forced to remain there. He would, with the greatest effort, tear himself away, saying with an excess of tender love: "Depart from me, O Lord depart!"

A Spanish Poor Clare loved to make visits to the Blessed Sacrament. Asked by the other nuns what she did during those long silent hours, she answered:

> I could kneel there forever. And why not? God is there! You wonder what I do in the presence of my God? I marvel, I love, I thank, I beg. What does a tramp do when he meets a millionaire? A sick man when he sees a doctor? A starving man when he sees food? What does a dry-throated hiker do at the drinking fountain?

St. Joseph Benedict LaBré, St. Paschal Baylon and St. Rose of Lima are three saints that we know of who spent forty straight hours in the presence of the Blessed Sacrament commemorating the forty hours Christ was in the tomb.

In the *Annals of Our Lady of Lourdes,* September, 1937, Fr. Markoe, pastor of St. Elizabeth's Church in St. Louis, Mo., told of an almost blind black woman named Daisy who

> on Holy Thursday was in the church at 6:00 in the morning. All day long, without moving, she knelt before the Blessed Sacrament. She never left the church. At Midnight I brought her in and insisted on her eating a sandwich and drinking some coffee. Then she went back and stayed all night. It was 4:00 in the afternoon of Good Friday that she finally left the church. She had been kneeling in prayer 34 hours.

So conscious were the saints of the awesome power and holiness of our Eucharistic Lord in the tabernacle that they were filled with a delight so complete that they were in a perpetual ecstasy while in His august presence. They made it a point to be their best in their appearance, demeanor and words.

St. Vincent Ferrer, St. Leonard of Port Maurice, St. Francis de Sales, and St. Francis of Assisi

St. Vincent Ferrer never came near the tabernacle unless he felt interior purity and was spotlessly clean on the outside. St. Leonard of Port Maurice said of St. Francis de Sales: "Never was there an ecclesiastic seen who stood before the altar with greater majesty, with greater awe, reverence and recollection." "Everything in man should halt in awe," said St. Francis of Assisi: "Let all the world quake and let heaven exult when Christ the Son of the living God is there on the altar."

The Imitation of Christ says,

> Many run to various places to visit relics of the saints, and are astonished to hear their wonderful works: they behold the noble church buildings and kiss their sacred bones, wrapped in silk and gold. And behold I have Thee here present on the altar, my God, the Saint of saints, the Creator of men, and the Lord of angels.

St. Alphonsus Liguori and Visits to the Blessed Sacrament

It is said that no other saint visited Jesus in the Eucharist as often as St. Alphonsus Liguori. He encouraged frequent visits to the Blessed Sacrament and wrote a treatise called *Visits to the Most Holy Sacrament of the Altar.* He was fond of repeating, "One thing is for certain, that next to Holy Communion, no act of worship is so pleasing to God, and none is so useful, as the daily visit to our Lord Jesus Christ in the Blessed Sacrament dwelling upon the altar."

St. John Vianney

St. John Vianney said: "Must we not say, with the Council of Trent, that His generosity and His magnanimity have here exhausted all His treasures? Is there anything on earth or in heaven which can be compared to it? Has the tender love of a father or the liberality of a king toward its subjects ever reached as far as the love of Jesus Christ in the Blessed Sacrament?"

Because of our wounded nature we are prone to discouragement. We experience pangs of emptiness and futility, our prayers seem cold and lifeless. But Eucharistic language is one of silent adoration where Christ speaks to the soul, listens to the heart, and understands what words can never say—and where silence was never more golden!

Abbot Marmion

Abbot Marmion tells us: "Once you feel the attraction to remain in the silence of adoration in God's presence, you must give yourself entirely to the Holy Spirit and remain there in pure faith. If God gives you no feeling, no sentiment, no distinct thought, just be there before Him in silent love. During such moments He operates insensibly in the soul and does more for her perfection than she could in a lifetime by her own thoughts."

Traveling hundreds of miles to feast their eyes upon the new born "King of kings," the three wise men of the Orient made the first visitation—a silent one.

Holy Hours & Eucharistic Adoration

The first Holy Hour was made by the Apostles—a silent one—as they watched with Christ when he went through His agony in the garden.

In His presence the heart always bears fruit, for a loving silence can enter more deeply into the heart than loving words, as was the experience of Pere Chaffangeon, an elderly peasant and parishioner of St. John Vianney's, who spent many hours in church in the presence of the Blessed Sacrament. One day St. John Vianney asked him: "Pere, what do you say to our Lord during your visits?" "I say nothing to Him; I look at Him, and He looks at me."

A new impetus was given to adoration of the Holy Eucharist when St. Alphonsus de Liquori introduced the custom of paying regular visits to our Lord hidden in the tabernacle. Since then numerous orders have devoted themselves to the unceasing adoration of the Blessed Sacrament. The devotion of "Perpetual Prayer" has been introduced into many dioceses to keep alive an ardent and devout faith in Him who said: "Behold I am with you all days, even to the consummation of the world."

Fr. Peter Maldonado

What a stunning contrast between Catholics who never bother to make a visit to the Blessed Sacrament and Fr. Peter Maldonado who died a martyr for the Blessed Sacrament during the time of the bloody persecution of the Church in Mexico. After his ordination to the priesthood, he established many pious organizations to increase devotion to the Blessed Sacrament in the different parishes he was assigned.

In 1926 the terrible Masonic persecution of the Church in Mexico erupted. Fr. Maldonado continued his priestly work during the ups and downs of these tragic times, all through the intense persecution under the Mexican President Calles, and into the presidency of Cardinas.

Fr. Maldonado spent many hours prostrate before the Blessed Sacrament, praying with his arms extended in the form of a cross. Because of the persecution, there were times when he could not go out but had to stay hidden indoors. At such times he had the opportunity to spend long hours in prayer and adoration before the Blessed Sacrament.

Martyr for the Eucharist

After many close calls, he was discovered. He hid the Blessed Sacrament in a pyx pressed against his chest. The soldiers beat him with the butts of their rifles and screamed at him to loosen his hands and give them "that thing in his chest." They yelled horrible blasphemies referring to the Eucharist. Fr. Maldonado grabbed the pyx very tightly in his hands, but his persecutors continued to blaspheme and yelled again and again, "Open the hand." By this time they had tortured him so badly that all of his teeth were broken, his left eye destroyed, his right arm fractured and a leg dislocated from the beatings with the rifle butts. Yet, in his agony, he held on tightly to the pyx to protect the Blessed Sacrament.

When the tormentors cut the cords of his hand with a knife, he no longer could protect the Blessed Sacrament and it fell to the floor. It is not clear what happened after that but sources have said there was a man in the room, still somewhat Catholic. He was frightened at what was going to happen to the Hosts, and picked them up and consumed them rather than see them desecrated.

Fr. John A. Hardon, S.J.

In his *Spiritual Life in the Modern World,* Fr. John Hardon, S.J., summed it all up in these words:

> It is impossible in human terms to exaggerate the importance of being in a church or chapel before the Blessed Sacrament as often and for as long as our duties and state of life allow. Let me repeat that sentence. It is impossible in human language to exaggerate the importance of being in a church or chapel before the Blessed Sacrament as often and for as long as our duties and state of life allow. That is the talisman of the highest sanctity.

3.
Holy Communion

Leon Dupont and Frequent Holy Communion

Called the "Holy Man of Tours," Leon Dupont was a man surrounded by all the comforts of modern life, and yet in the depths of his soul he was almost without feeling for the pleasures and honors of the world.

Modern times have need of outstanding laymen. Leon was a model of a Christian father in a time which was weak in faith and charity. Highly educated and affluent, he moved in the best circles of society, and combined the polish of a man of the world with the solid principles of a saint.

He was, above all, an advocate of frequent Holy Communion. Again and again, he dwelt upon it in private conversation and in his letters. "The Christian without Holy Communion," he said, "is a fish out of water." He wrote a pamphlet under the title: "Faith and Piety Regenerated in the Mystery of the Eucharist."

I Live Now not I, But Christ Lives in Me The more humble and patient, pure and kind we are, the greater the depth of our union with Jesus in Holy Communion. And the more intimate we become with Jesus in the Holy Eucharist, the more the fire of divine love will inflame our heart, illumine our mind, and cleanse the dross from our soul, exciting us to greater strides in imitating Him. With each conscious reception of Holy Communion, we are led from darkness to light, from mediocrity to perfection as the life-blood of Christ, and the fruits accompanying it, are applied to us to the extent we open ourselves to His grace. His Sacred Heart can become the heart of our heart, His Soul the soul of our soul so that when we speak, it will be Christ; when we listen, it will be Christ; when we love, it will be Christ; when we pray, it will be Christ. And with St. Paul, we too can say: "I live now not I, but Christ lives in me."

St. John Chrysostom Called "The Doctor of the Eucharist," St. John Chrysostom, in one of the most forceful passages in his writings, said:

> How many in these times say: would that I could gaze upon His form, His figure; His garment, His shoes! Lo! Thou seest Him, touchest Him, eatest Him. He gives Himself to thee, not merely to look upon, but even to touch, to eat, and to receive within.... Consider at Whose table thou eatest! For we are fed with

> that which the angels view with trepidation and which they cannot contemplate without fear because of its splendor. We become one with Him; we become one body and one flesh with Christ.

When the Saracens captured St. Louis X, the fearless 13th century crusader and the king of France, they held all of France for ransom; likewise with Jesus in the confines of our heart, we already possess heaven!

No doubt, volumes could be written containing statements the saints and holy people have made about the effects of Holy Communion. Here are some of the more notable:

"By the humble, frequent, and devout reception of the Eucharist, a person will progress more speedily in divine union and holiness of life than by any other exercise." **Abbot Blosius**

"Each time a person receives Holy Communion, their place in heaven becomes greater and their stay in purgatory is shortened." **St. Gertrude**

"This food strengthens us little or much, according to the desire of him who receives it, in whatever way hc may receive it." **St. Catherine of Siena**

"It is the medicine of immortality." **St. Ignatius**

St. Pius X "Holy Communion is the shortest and surest way to heaven."

St. Francis de Sales "Nowhere do we find our Savior more tender or more loving than here where He, so to speak, annihilates Himself and reduces Himself to food in order to penetrate our souls and to unite Himself to the hearts of His friends."

St. Lawrence Justinian "You have willed, O God enamored of our souls, that by means of this sacrament Your heart and our heart should become but one heart inseparably united."

St. John Chrysostom "Jesus, for the burning love He bore us, wished to unite Himself so closely to us that we should become one and the same with Him for such is the dream of true lovers."

Pope John Paul II "The Holy Eucharist contains the entire spiritual treasure of the Church, that is, Christ Himself, our passover and living bread."

Pope Leo XIII "The Eucharist, as it were, is the soul of the Church."

St. John Vianney "Of all the Sacraments, there is not one that can be compared to the Holy Eucharist...a soul may receive its Creator, and as often as it desires."

"The Eucharist is the supreme proof of the love of Jesus. Afer this, there is nothing more but heaven....Be willing to sacrifice everything, be willing to do everything for the sake of one communion. A single communion is able to transform a sinner into a saint instantaneously, because it is Jesus Christ Himself, author of all sanctity, who comes to you." **St. Peter Julian Eymard**

"The Eucharist is the sacrament of love: it signifies love, it produces love." **St. Thomas Aquinas**

"The most sanctifying action a Christian can perform is to receive Christ in the Eucharistic mystery." **Thomas Merton**

"Each Communion takes us further and further into the infinite abyss of the Divinity." **Abbot Marmion**

"Be convinced that there is in all your life no more precious time than that of Holy Communion and the moments following, during which you have the happiness to be able to speak face to face, heart to heart, with Jesus." **St. John Baptist de las Salle**

"The Eucharist is that love which surpasses all loves in Heaven and on earth." **St. Bernard**

Fr. Lawrence G. Lovasik	"In all other sacraments we receive the grace of Christ, but in this sacrament we receive Christ Himself."
St. Gemma Galgani	"It is not possible to have a union of love more profound and more total: He in me and I in Him; the one in the other. What more could we want?"
St. Madeleine Sophie Barat	"Holy Communion is paradise on earth."
St. Ignatius Loyola	"Of the gifts of grace which the soul receives in the Eucharist, one must be counted among the highest; the Eucharist does not allow the soul to remain long in sin or to persist in it obstinately."
Bishop Fulton J. Sheen	"The Eucharist is the point where God and the soul meet—God with all His graces, the soul with all its wants."
St. Mary Magdalen of Pazzi	"Sacrifice all earthly goods rather than a single communion."
Fr. Stephano Manelli	"In Holy Communion, Jesus gives Himself to me and becomes mine, all mine, in His Body, Blood, Soul and Divinity."

"There is no greater aid to holiness than frequent communion. How marvelously the Lord shows His power therein." **St. Teresa of Avila**

"Two kinds of people should communicate frequently: the perfect to stay perfect, the imperfect to become perfect." **St. Alphonsus de Liguori**

"Holy Communion makes us eager for virtue and prompt to practice it, at the same time imparting deep peace, and thus rendering sweet and easy the road to holiness." **St. John Chrysostom**

"The Sacrament of the Eucharist is far more powerful for the sanctification of souls than all other spiritual means of grace." **St. Denis**

"The best means to reach perfection is through receiving Holy Communion frequently. Experience sufficiently proves it in those who practice it." **St. Therese of Lisieux**

"Among the thousands of young men whom I have directed I do not know of even one whom I saved uncorrupted unless he went to Holy Communion every two weeks; and the numerous others, whom I could not save, nearly all had to ascribe their fall to the neglect of the Sacraments." **St. John Nepomucene Neumann**

Jesus Christ "My Flesh is food indeed and My Blood is drink indeed."

St. Joseph Moscati: Eucharistic Doctor St. Joseph Moscati was canonized by Pope John Paul II on October 25, 1987 amidst a crown of 80,000 who attended Mass, which was concelebrated by 25 bishops and 2 cardinals. Since he was only 47 years of age when he died, people were astounded at the souls he was responsible for saving by caring for the body as a medical doctor. To someone who asked how he managed to cope with his demanding and busy schedule, he replied: "By the daily reception of Jesus in the Sacrament of the Holy Eucharist."

Receiving Jesus in Holy Communion is greater than having Him make a personal visit to our home. What preparations we make to welcome a guest into our home! Everything must be in order, the house spotless, and an air of harmony and happiness, peace and joy, must be presented to our guest to make him or her feel welcome. What preparations would one make to welcome the governor of the State into one's home because of his station in life, his dignity of office? How much more so would one welcome the President of the United States because of his greater station in life, his greater dignity of office? What preparation would one make to receive the Holy Father the Pope, the vicar of Christ on earth, the most important office in the world? How much more, therefore, if our Lord were to come into our homes, He who loved us to life! This, then, can be a gauge of how we should prepare ourselves to receive our Lord in the Holy Eucharist. The reception of Jesus into our souls is so intimate and so sacred that no words can describe this visit. Hence it is called Holy Communion.

The saintly Abbot Marmion was so fully aware of this that he told one of his correspondents: "I have now divided my day into two parts: (1) I live on my morning Communion; (2) I prepare for the next."

Scott Hahn's Conversion

The former Protestant minister, Scott Hahn, tells how, out of consuming curiosity,

> I went to Mass one day. I sat there looking at all these people. I looked at their devotion, their sincerity taking time out in the middle of the day to worship; and I watched how, during the consecration, their heads were lowered, their lips were moving, their hearts were stirring. I went back the next day, and the next, and the next. Within a week or two I had fallen head over heels in love with the Mass. I was transformed. The Eucharist became, in a sense, the all-controlling central desire of my life! I can't describe to you the passionate thirst and hunger that came over me day after day as I saw all of these people going up and being fed with the Body and Blood of our Lord!

Our Lord made no statement in regards to how often we ought to receive Holy Communion, but He implied that we ought to receive often for He compared the Eucharist to the manna that was the daily meal of the Jews wandering in the desert.

Vatican II and the Council of Trent

In its Decree on Daily Holy Communion, the Sacred Congregation of the Council expressly declares:

> The desire of Jesus Christ and of the Church that all the faithful should daily approach the sacred banquet is directed chiefly to this end, that the faithful, being united to God by means of the sacrament, may thence derive strength to resist their sensual passions, to cleanse themselves from the stains of daily faults, and to avoid those graver sins to which human frailty is liable so that its primary purpose is not that the honor and reverence due to our Lord may be safeguarded, or that the Sacrament may serve as a reward of virtue bestowed on the recipients. Hence the holy Council of Trent calls the Eucharist "the antidote whereby we are delivered from daily faults and preserved from deadly sins."

St. Thomas: The Power of the Eucharist

Daily Holy Communion is the supreme remedy against temptation. And there is no habit, no matter how strong it is, that can withstand the tremendous power this sacrament delivers. St. Thomas Aquinas said:

> The Sacrament of the Body of the Lord puts the demons to flight, defends us against the incentives to vice and to concupiscence, cleanses the soul from sin, assuages the anger of God, enlightens the understanding to know God, inflames the will and the affection with the love of God, fills the memory with spiritual sweetness, confirms the entire man in good, frees us from eternal death, multiplies the merits of a good life, leads us to our everlasting home, and reanimates the body to eternal life.

Holy Communion, daily if possible, brings the most perfect union with Jesus that is possible in this life, and receiving Him into our souls works wonders. We can attain to the heights of sanctity which Christ has intended for us. Frequently Holy Communion withdraws one from evil and enhances our pathway to holiness. It is the food for the strong; it is the food for the weak.

4.
Source of Unity

Failed Efforts at Human Unity

In committing the first sin, Adam and Eve broke off their communication with God; and, because they listened to the Prince of Darkness, darkness followed immediately. They ignored the "voice forever sounding across the centuries the laws of right and wrong" and listened to the creature rather than the Creator, heeded the secular rather than the Eternal and succumbed to the inwardly directed goal of self-fulfillment. The great deceiver expressed the Divine command as one of servility and jealousy. Confusion and contention has been part and parcel of man's life ever since, and the tower of Babel with its divisive effects repeats itself in today's world.

Man has sought from time immemorial, through the League of Nations after the First World War, and United Nations after the Second World War, to set aside all differences, to work in harmony, to become one family. However, an excessive love of materialism and self-love, lust for prestige and money obstruct the view of man, who all to often denies the Creator to please the creature, exchanging the 10 Commandments for 30 pieces of silver.

Housed in a body, dulled by the whims and desires of the senses, held captive by time, the soul unconsciously craves the Bread of heaven—its fuel to attain its goal in this life and immortality in the next.

The Bread of Love

In the early church, what was considered burdensome was borne in patience and joy, and what was considered an imposition was accepted in loving obedience, because the creature was nourished with the heavenly Bread that is God Who is Love. Hence, the mark of the early Christians was love: "See how those Christians love one another!" The Greek word *koinonia* meant: communion and community through the Eucharist—the Bread of Love.

In his book *Apostolic Renewal,* Fr. Luke Zimmer, SS.CC., said: "The presence of Christ in the Blessed Sacrament is a constant reminder of the permanent presence of Christ in His Church to maintain it in unity."

Unity in Christ

All barriers of nationality, social status, education, wealth, professional positions and personal preferences are dropped on ocean liners with the ringing of a bell announcing the beginning of Mass.

Side by side kneel the high and low, rich and poor, educated and uneducated, white and brown, young and old, Americans, Canadians, French, British, Germans, Belgians, Poles, Italians and Russians. They have no tongue in common but that of Mother Church. They are united through the Holy Sacrifice of the Mass, and a universal faith that Christ is truly present in the Holy Eucharist. Here is an unconscious unity without the loss of individuality.

Protestants on the Catholic Church

It is remarkable what Protestant ministers have had to say about the unity and continuity of the Catholic Church through the Holy Sacrifice of the Mass which make the Holy Eucharist possible: "The providential purpose of the Roman Catholic Church is unity and continuity," said the Rev. J. S., Thompson of the Independent Church of Los Angeles, California. He continued,

> The Catholic Church is the grandest organization in the world. It has a place of consecrated duty for all types or groups of mind. The poor, the common, and the rich meet together in that Church, as children of the same common Father. The poor, hard-working man and woman are found in that Church....It has cohesion and unity and continuity.

The very fact of its great age is proof of its providential purpose.

The Rev. James Benninger, a Methodist of Wilkes-Barre, Pa., said:

> The reason the Catholic Church succeeds, in spite of our misgivings, is because she is true to the central fact of revelation. She makes the death of Jesus the center of her devotion, around that point she organizes all her activities. When you see a company of Catholic people on the way to church, you can be assured of this....They are going to that place of worship to attend Mass. What is the celebration of the Mass? It is what we call the celebration of the Lord's Supper. That fact is kept prominently before the mind of every Catholic.

Rev. Dr. T. Moffatt, a Congregationalist of Newark, N.J., said: "What do I admire about the Catholic Church? ...the central unifying authority of the Church."

Christ's Plan for Unity

It is Christ's plan that all become one. "And other sheep I have that are not of this fold. Them also I must bring, and they shall hear My voice and there shall be one fold and one shepherd" (John 10:16). There can be one body, as there is, in reality, but one bread. But only a bread from heaven, the Holy Eucharist, can unify.

Christ's grace does everything, but He uses us as His envoys. Many have heard His "voice" through observing the virtuous example of others, and have found this a thing to be greatly desired and advantageous. People do not like to be preached to, but shown by example. Actions speak a language every one can appreciate and apply. A marvelous instance of not only the example—and the unity—but the strength that Holy Communion gives, is the conversion of the famed coach of Notre Dame, Knute Rockne.

Knute Rockne

"I used to be deeply impressed at the sight of my players receiving communion every morning," he said, "and finally I made it a point of going to Mass with them on the morning of a game."

> I realized that it appeared more or less incongruous, when we arrived in town for a game, for the general public to see my boys rushing off to church as soon as they got off the train, while their coach rode to the hotel and took his ease. So for the sake of appearances, if nothing else, I made it a point to go to church with the boys on the morning of a game.
>
> One night before a big game in the east, I was nervous and worried about the outcome of the game the next day and was unable to sleep. I tossed and rolled about the bed, and finally decided that I'd get up and dress, then go down to the lobby and sit in a chair and tried to get

that football game off my mind by engaging some bellboys in conversation.

Along about five or six o'clock in the morning I started pacing the lobby of the hotel; when suddenly I ran into two of my players hurrying out. I asked them where they were going at such an hour, although I had a good idea.

Then I retired to a chair in the corner of the lobby where I couldn't be seen, but where I could see everyone who went in or out of the door. Within the next few minutes, my players kept hurrying out of the door in pairs and groups, and finally when they were all gone, I got over near the door so I could question the next player who came along. In a minute or two, the last members of the squad hurried out of an elevator and made for the door. I stopped them and asked them if they, too, were going to Mass, and they replied that they were. I decided to go along with them.

Although they probably didn't realize it, these youngsters were making a powerful impression on me with their piety and devotion, and when I saw all of them walking up to the communion rail to receive, and realized the several hours' sleep they had sacrificed in order to do this, I understood for the first time what a powerful ally their religion was to those boys in their work on the football field. This was when I really began to see the light, to know what was missing in my life, and, later on, I had the great pleasure of being able to join my boys at the Communion rail.

Banishing Hatred and Enmity

The Holy Eucharist has to be received with deep, heartfelt sincerity in order to really experience the unlimited power it has to banish hatred and enmity and to keep us from nursing habitual grudges and dislikes, the jealousy and envy which so often is the cause of division among us. "Some of us would be surprised," said St. Ignatius Loyola, "if they knew what God could make of them if, in the decisive moments of their lives, they gave ear to the voice of grace!" And, certainly, one of these decisive moments is the time that Christ dwells in us in Holy Communion, for God works a profusion of miracles in the Eucharist. Nowhere are the attributes of God so radiantly manifested as in his mystery. It is the greatest means of transforming a soul into the likeness of Christ, and it is the most excellent of God's gifts, giving us the most wonderful characteristics of love, forgiveness, peace and reconciliation.

St. Maria Goretti

A powerful example of this happened on July 6, 1902, in Corinaldo, Italy, when little Maria Goretti, twelve years of age, was found by her mother lying on the kitchen floor in a pool of blood, dying from the fourteen wounds the teenager, Alexander

Serenelli, had inflicted upon her body with a butcher knife because she would not consent to his immoral wishes—fueled by pornographic books and pictures which he kept in his bedroom.

Maria was a very beautiful child, full of love for God and her family; everyone remarked upon the sweetness and purity of her disposition, the joy and fervor of her prayer. Only God can know the nightmare, the agony, the grief her poor mother experienced. Maria was the joy of her life.

Rushed to a hospital in a horse and wagon over rough roads, the discomfort of the hard, bouncy ride intensified her pain. At the hospital a priest, Fr. Signori, was called to anoint her. After administering to her, his eyes moist with tears, he asked her if she forgave Alexander for what he did. Because of the difficulty breathing, her life slowly ebbing away, in a low voice she said to the priest: "Yes, yes! I forgive him with all my heart. I want him to be with me in heaven." Maria died within twenty hours.

Alexander received a thirty-year prison sentence. While in prison, he was changed one night from a hardened, incorrigible prisoner to a meek and repentant soul when Maria appeared to him in his cell saying she forgave him.

Alexander Serenelli and Assunta Goretti

Alexander became a model prisoner. Upon his release from prison he went to see Maria's mother, Assunta, to beg her forgiveness. Assunta was eating supper when she heard the rap on the door. Opening the door she was stunned to see Alexander. Before he could say a word, she said to him: "Come in son," and after giving him a warm embrace, shared a meal with him. In the morning they were at Mass receiving Holy Communion together. She told him that "if Maria can forgive you, so can I."

Because Assunta Goretti saw God in the Holy Eucharist, she was able to see Christ in Alexander, confirming that the sacrament of the Eucharist is the food of love and unity which demands faith and devotion of believers to obtain its full effectiveness.

Assunta indeed, as Pope Pius XII was to indicate on the day of Maria's canonization, was of bearing no less heroic than her daughter. Both Assunta and Alexander were present at the canonization of Maria which was the first time in history of the church that a parent witnessed her child raised to the honors of sanctity.

Pope Pius XII

On August 15, 1927, at the Eucharistic Congress in Bologna, Italy, Pope Pius XII said: "Everyone knows how much good is gained by the individual and the community when when the faithful as a whole have a deeper knowledge of the Eucharist and live according to its precepts."

It is important to realize that the fruits we receive are in proportion to the disposition in which we receive. Acts of faith and love, and wanting Christ to change us, give us the proper disposition. Due to our fallen nature, we tend to see the outside where Christ sees the inside; we see the motion where Christ sees the motive.

The Law of Love of God and Neighbor

The eminent theologian, Francisco Suarez, says: "The Holy Eucharist has for its primary and direct effect to nourish charity solely for its own perfection and a more intimate union with Christ."

The Jews had 613 laws that they had to abide by. One such law said that you could not pluck a fruit from your neighbor's tree, stand there, and eat it. However, it was permissible to pluck the fruit and eat it as long as you continued walking in the process.

When the Jewish lawyer asked Jesus which was the greatest of all the laws, our Lord answered: "You shall love the Lord your God with all of your heart, with all of your soul, with all of your strength and with all of your will." And, He said, "The second is like unto it. You shall love your neighbor as yourself."

The saints ate, walked, talked, listened, prayed and slept those profound words. It was their goal to master Christ's words.

And because they had mastered loving God to such an extent that they were able to see Him in the Eucharist, they were able to see Christ in their neighbor, for belief opens the doors to love. One would be greatly challenged to find a greater example of this love than that of Fr. Damien. Known world wide as "Damien the Leper," Fr. Damien can still fire the imagination and move others to action even though he lived one hundred years ago. In this age of unbelief and self-seeking, he is an example of extraordinary heroism and of so sublime a character that even the most degenerate men must admire him.

Damien of Molokai

He arrived on Molokai, called the island of "dread and death," with a resolve of giving himself without reserve to the eight hundred poor lepers to administer to their spiritual and bodily needs. He would become their counselor, physician, priest, judge, sheriff, builder, carpenter, undertaker and grave-digger. He bathed their wounds and bandaged their sores. He didn't shrink when they sprayed him with spittle as he heard their confessions. He gave them what they needed most: respect and love. He fought immorality, drunkenness and lawlessness which he found among the adult lepers when he arrived. In twelve years he would build three hundred houses and make one thousand coffins. With unwearying patience he had given the consolations of religion to the most destitute people in the world.

On November 25, 1873, he wrote of the hopeless exile and dull despair of these poor souls:

> Even the breath of the lepers is so foul-smelling that the air is tainted with it. It comes hard on me to live in this atmosphere. One day while I was celebrating Mass, I thought I would suffocate and I was almost unable to restrain myself from rushing out to take a breath of fresh air. But the thought of my Lord before the grave of Lazarus restored me. My sense of smell is already somewhat dulled, so that it is not quite so hard for me to enter the pestilent dwelling-rooms of the poor sick people. Of course, there comes upon me now and then a feeling of loathing, especially when I must hear the confessions of the sick whose wounds are already full of worms similar to those which consume bodies in the grave. I have often been in great perplexity when I wished to give Extreme Unction because there was not to be found free space between the wounds. There are no physicians here, in fact they could be of no use.

The Source of His Strength

An Anglican minister who wrote Fr. Damien asked what was the secret of his strength for such heroic work. Fr. Damien answered: "The continued presence of Christ in the Blessed Sacrament and the daily reception of the Holy Eucharist alone gave me the strength to endure."

Hence would St. Augustine speak, "O Sacrament of love, O sign of unity, O bond of charity." And St. Thomas Aquinas: "The Eucharist is the unity of the Church—the body of Christ—in charity."

5.
Spiritual Gems

Fulton Sheen

"One cannot get close enough to the fire without being ignited." The fire of Archbishop Fulton J. Sheen's enthusiasm and the magnetic appeal of his oration had its source in daily holy hours. He was persistent in urging others to make holy hours before the Blessed Sacrament, where he learned from his master the secret of winning converts: "Kindness, more kindness, most kindness," which holds the key to every heart.

Msgr. Escriva

To a person worried and sad because his communions were cold and barren, Msgr. Josemaria Escriva, founder of Opus Dei, said: "Tell me, when you approach the sacrament, do you seek yourself, or do you seek Jesus? If you seek yourself, there is reason indeed to be sad. But if you seek Christ—as you ought—could you want a surer sign than the cross to know you've found Him?"

Fr. William Doyle In the letter to a woman having troubles making visits to the Blessed Sacrament, Fr. William Doyle, S.J., wrote "Real devotion to the Blessed Sacrament is only to be gained by hard, grinding work of dry adoration before the hidden God. But such a treasure cannot be purchased at too great a cost, for once obtained it makes of this life as near an approach to heaven as we can hope for."

St. Clement Hofbauer Called "The Apostle of Vienna," St. Clement Hofbauer found his strength in the Blessed Sacrament. Opening an orphanage, he collected alms to maintain it. On one of his begging expeditions, a man who was playing cards in a tavern replied to his appeal by spitting in his face. Clement, wiping the spittle from his face with his handkerchief and smiling, said to the man: "Thank you sir. That was for me; now would you please give me something for the poor?" This is strength indeed!

Cardinal Vaughn Cardinal Vaughn of London often related the following story. A Protestant minister, who by the grace of God was powerfully drawn towards Catholicism, but could not resolve to take the decisive step, had come to London. He was the father of a family, and was accompanied by his five-year-old daughter.

He took the child first into a Catholic Church where her attention was immediately attracted by the perpetual lamp which burned before the tabernacle.

"Papa, why is that lamp burning there?"

"That signifies that Jesus is in this church, just behind the little golden door which you see upon the altar." Later they entered a Protestant Church, where there was neither lamp nor tabernacle.

"Papa, why is there no lamp here?"

"Because Jesus is not here."

Pondering the conversation with his daughter, he and his family later embraced the true religion, especially from hearing his daughter repeat, over and over, "I want to go where Jesus is."

St. John Vianney: God in a Man

A man struggling with faith was challenged to see John Vianney. Later, upon being asked if he had seen him, he replied: "No, I did not see John Vianney. I saw God in a man!"

St. John Vianney opened himself up to God's grace to such an extent that he was transformed into an image of the invisible God.

St. Jerome

While St. Jerome resided at Rome in the time of Pope Damasus, in 384, he spent long periods of time in prayer before the

Eucharist after Mass. The wisdom he gained from this may be illustrated by his shrewd admonition regarding the loose morals of the city of Rome, and admonition still most appropriate today: "Man is paper, woman fire, Satan the wind."

St. Teresa of Avila St. Teresa of Avila said that in this world it is impossible for all subjects to speak to the king, and they must do so by way of a third party. "But to speak with Thee, O King of heaven, there is no need of a third person for everyone that wishes can find Thee in the most Blessed Sacrament."

St. Francis Jerome St. Francis Jerome had two great interests: "family communions" which he organized city wide, and preaching sermons outdoors to those unaccustomed to frequenting churches. His sermons were well-planned, short, energetic. He was so moved by Christ's words: "What does it profit a man if he gain the whole world and suffer the loss of his soul," that he searched everywhere to find sinners to convert. His sermons stressed personal conviction of sin. He preached in alleys, on street corners, on the city docks and on the decks of prison ships in the harbor of Naples. He used every means to win hearts to conversion, often holding a skull aloft while he spoke. He insisted that a loss of the sense of sin was a loss of the sense of God.

In Tune with the Divine Musician

After a spell-binding performance in Carnegie Hall, a woman, all excited, burst into the presence of the great violinist, Fritz Kreisler, and said to him: "Mr. Kreisler, if I could play like that I'd give twenty years of my life!" Mr. Kreisler replied: "Lady, I did!"

We may not become a Fritz Kreisler but we can become a holy person by spending time in the presence of the "Holy of Holies." There we will learn the music of God—silence—and we will know its echo which is spiritual power that keeps one in tune and in perfect harmony with the Divine Musician. And one day, we can become like the instrument of the mystic Hazrat Kahn, who summed up his life by saying, "I played the flute until my heart turned into the same instrument. Then I offered this instrument to the Divine Musician. Since then, I have become His flute, and when He chooses He plays."

St. Ignatius Loyola

A tremendous lover of Jesus in the Blessed Sacrament, St. Ignatius Loyola, used to say: "Pray like everything depends on God; work like everything depends on you."

St. Augustine and St. John Vianney on Humility

St. Augustine said people were foolish seeking satisfaction in worldly things. He urged people to come to Christ in the Blessed Sacrament, who alone can satisfy the cravings of their hearts. Before the Blessed

Sacrament he received untold inspirations. "Humility," he said,

> is the foundation of all the virtues; therefore, in a soul where it does not exist, there can be no true virtue, but the mere appearance only. In like manner, it is the most proper disposition for all celestial gifts. And, finally, it is so necessary to perfection, that of all the ways to reach it, the first is humility; the second, humility; the third, humility. And if the question were repeated a hundred times, I should always give the same answer.

The Eucharistic adorer, St. John Vianney, patron saint of parish priests, echoes St. Augustine: "Humility is to the various virtues what the chain is to the Rosary; take away the chain and the beads are scattered, remove humility and all virtues vanish."

Matt Talbot, the Saint in Overalls

Know as "The Saint in Overalls," Matt Talbot was as common a sight as a kneeling figure on church steps and in the churches. His religious spirit was exceptional. He used to kneel outside of the locked doors of the church at 4:00 a.m. waiting for the doors to be opened at 6:00 a.m. Upon entering, he would prostrate himself upon the floor in the form of a cross before going to his place. Except when he went to Holy Communion, he would kneel through the entire Mass, even during the Gospel. On Sundays he would stay in church, without moving, for seven hours, his eyes shut, his bare knees (he slit his trousers lengthwise for added penance) pressed into the hard wooden kneelers, his arms crossed, his elbows not resting on anything, his body from the knees up as rigid and straight as the candles burning in adoration on the altar. This was his practice for nearly forty years!

"God wants constancy," Matt said. And Matt's incredible constancy was enhanced by his constantly pondering "the eye of God, the voice of conscience, and the stroke of death," the three things which he said no man can escape.

Upon hearing in a sermon that "in giving us a free-will, God gave us a choice of three options: to be a saint, a devil, a fool," a man vowed to make as many holy hours before the Blessed Sacrament as he could for the remainder of his life.

Three Springs of the Supernatural Life

Known as a visionary, author, founder of two religious orders, a reader of hearts, a foreteller of future events, and a miracle worker, St. John Bosco often spoke of three "springs" of the supernatural life: Confession, devotion to the Blessed Virgin Mary, and the reception of Holy Communion.

Known as "The sun of theological schools," St. Thomas Aquinas wrote most eloquently of the Blessed Sacrament. How profoundly he would look at the Blessed Sacrament and say: "Touch, taste and sight in Thee are each deceived; the ear alone most safely is believed."

Knowing of his great intimacy with our Lord in the Blessed Sacrament, his sister asked him: "What must I do to become a saint?" He replied in but two words: "Will it!"

Fr. Doyle, Soldier of the Eucharist

Fr. William Doyle, S.J., was a chaplain in World War One for the Irish soldiers fighting in France. His furlough time back in Ireland would find him before the Blessed Sacrament spending entire nights. On one occasion he entered a church late at night and thought he was alone. In the back of the church was another priest who saw Fr. Doyle walk up to the tabernacle, wrap his arms around it, and say over and over: "Oh Jesus, I love you!" What was it that spurred this holy priest on? He himself shares the secret with us in his book *Joy For Every Tomorrow:*

> I can imagine I am a soul in hell, and God in His mercy is saying to me, "Return to the world for this year and on your manner of life during the year will depend your returning to hell or not." What a life I should lead! How little I should think of suffering, of mortification! How I would rejoice in suffering! How perfectly each moment would be spent!

St. Anthony of Padua on Hell

Hell is real—it does exist. When St. Anthony of Padua was giving the eulogy at the funeral for a very prominent citizen of the city, he shocked the congregation by proclaiming that the man had gone to hell, and he proceeded to admonish the people to change their ways in order to avoid a similar fate.

St. Anthony Claret

St. Anthony Mary Claret had always been especially attracted by devotions honoring the Blessed Sacrament. During his school days he had been so captivated by a book his father gave him, *The Goodness of Our Sacramental Lord,* that he had committed it to memory!

Kneeling before the Blessed Sacrament, he would pray: "Oh my God, grant me a place by the gates of hell, that I may stop those who enter there, saying: 'Where are you going, unhappy one? Back, go back! Make a good confession. Save your soul! Don't come back here to be lost forever'."

Abbot Blosius

Abbot Blosius spent all of his spare moments visiting our Lord in the Blessed Sacrament, where, no doubt, he received his inspiration to write his classic book, *A Book of Spiritual Instruction.* To encourage people to love God, he said, "For a soul that loves God to go to hell involves a contradiction."

St. John of the Cross

St. John of the Cross, who practically became one with Jesus in the Blessed Sacrament, said: "To restrain the tongue and the thoughts, and to set the affections regularly upon God, quickly sets the soul on fire in a divine way."

St. Peter Julian Eymard and Eucharistic Spirituality

Perhaps no one has spoken or written so insistently on the Holy Eucharist as St. Peter Julian Eymard. The Eucharistic approach to the problems of the soul is his distinctive spirituality. He looked upon an hour of adoration before the Blessed Sacrament as an hour in Paradise! "Go to your adoration as one would to heaven!" His great ambition was to lead souls to the Blessed Sacrament,

> Because in communion we receive the glorified Body of Christ, we receive more than Mary received in the Incarnation. The Body Mary carried in her womb was simply the human Body of the Savior; we receive His impassible, celestial Body. Mary carried the man of sorrows; we carry the Son of God crowned with glory!

St. Francis de Sales' Secret of Spiritual Growth

Of St. Francis de Sales, St. Vincent de Paul said: "Oh my God! How good must Thou be, since the Bishop of Geneva is so good!" From Sacramental Communion his soul advanced in grace and naturally passed on to spiritual communion, and thus his life became one continuous communion with Christ. He was accustomed to say that when we pray for the suffering souls, whom he said we do not remember enough, we perform the other thirteen works of mercy. "Is it not," he said,

> in some manner, to visit the sick, to obtain by our prayers the relief of the poor suffering souls in purgatory? Is it not to give drink to those who thirst after the vision of God, and who are enveloped in burning flames, to share with them the dew of our prayers? Is it not to feed the hungry, to aid in their deliverance by the means which faith suggests? Is it not to clothe the naked, to procure for them a garment of light, a raiment of glory? Is it not an admirable degree of hospitality to procure their admission into heavenly Jerusalem, and to make them fellow-citizens with the saints of God? Is it not a greater service to place souls in heaven, than to bury bodies in the earth?
>
> As to the Spiritual works, is it not a work whose merit may be compared to that of counseling the weak, correcting the wayward, instructing the ignorant, forgiving offenses, enduring injuries? And what consolation, however great, that can be given to the afflicted of this world, is comparable with that which is wrought by our prayers, to those poor souls who have such bitter need of them?

Fr. Frederick William Faber

And the great spiritual writer, Fr. Frederick Faber, whose book *The Blessed Sacrament* is a classic, affirmed St. Francis de Sales' statement: "There is no greater charity than praying for the poor souls in purgatory. This work constitutes the highest charity we can perform and is the summation of all charity. Hence, in God's eyes, it is the most pleasing charity we can perform."

St. Franics of Assisi: My Lord and My God

It is doubtful that the love St. Francis of Assisi had for the Creator and the created has ever been surpassed. The intense fire of love that consumed him generated waves of warmth and kindness that were infectious, melting hearts. He spent entire nights before the Blessed Sacrament burning with love for Jesus, saying over and over, all night long, "My Lord and my God."

He once said to a brother: "Come, let us go preach a sermon." St. Francis, with the brother following close behind, walked through a town without saying a word, turned around and walked out, returning to the monastery. "I thought we were going to preach a sermon," said the brother. St. Francis replied: "We did!"

Blessed Kateri Tekakwitha

Known as "The Lily of the Mohawks," Blessed Kateri Tekakwitha, which translates "She-who-feels-her-way-along," was so named because of her weakness of vision due to a smallpox disease. She made her first Holy Communion on Christmas Day, 1677, and from that time on advanced rapidly on the road to holiness.

At 4:00 a.m. she could be seen kneeling outside the chapel in the snow waiting for it to open. She attended three Masses daily, and always managed two hours in preparation for Holy Communion and two hours in thanksgiving; and she made frequent visits to the Blessed Sacrament. Her motto was: "Who will teach me what is most agreeable to God so that I may do it?"

Bl. Crescentia of Kaufbeuren & St. Elizabeth Ann Seton

As if in imitation of Blessed Kateri, Blessed Crescentia of Kaufbeuren often said: "Two things constitute my heaven on earth: The Holy Will of God and the Most Blessed Sacrament." Likewise, St. Elizabeth Ann Seton found great repose, holy peace, knowledge of self, spiritual contentment and complete submission to God's will in the presence of the Blessed Sacrament. "What was the first rule of our Savior's life?" she asked. "You know it was to do the Father's will. Well, then, the first purpose of our daily work is to do the will of God; secondly, to do it in the manner He wills; thirdly, to do it because it is His will."

St. Thomas More

St. Thomas More well understood this subordination of man's will to the will of God in the Eucharist. When he was questioned about serving Mass, with the suggestion that

King Henry would be displeased by his lowering himself to do so, he replied: "My king cannot be displeased at the homage I offer his King."

6.
It Is Jesus

St. Bernadette and Our Lady

On June 3, 1858, the day after her first Holy Communion, less than four months after our Lady had appeared to her for the first time, a friend of Bernadette's said to her: "Tell me, which of the two things was the greatest joy to you, the receiving of your God in Holy Communion, or conversing with the Blessed Virgin at the grotto?" Bernadette hesitated momentarily, and then replied: "I do not know; the two things go together and cannot be compared. All I know is that I was intensely happy in them both."

Bernadette gave an excellent answer, for was not the flesh of Christ taken from Mary's body and His Blood taken from Hers?

Genuine devotion to Mary inevitably leads to Jesus in the Blessed Sacrament! Jesus could not give us His Body to eat in the Eucharist until Mary had first given Him that Body.

The word Eucharist is a Greek word which means "thanksgiving." Because Christ offered a prayer of thanksgiving when He consecrated the bread and wine at the Last Supper, the word has always been connected with the Sacrament of the Lord's Supper.

St. Peter Damian

"As Eve," said St. Peter Damian, "induced man to eat of the forbidden fruit which brought death upon us, so it is right that Mary should prompt us to eat the Bread which gives us life."

The word "lady" is derived from the Anglo-Saxon "laef-da," which means "loaf-giver" or "bread-giver"; and Bethlehem, where Mary gave birth to Jesus, is a Hebrew word which means "place of food!"

In John 6:51, Christ says: "I am the living bread that came down from heaven; whoever eats this bread will live forever; and the bread that I will give is my flesh for the life of the world."

Real Flesh, Sacramentally

One of the questions asked of Frs. Rumble and Carty of Radio Replies fame was: "Are you not guilty of cannibalism?" Their answer:

> No, Catholics do not believe that they are eating Christ's human flesh in its

> natural form. There is a change of substance and nothing else in the Host. The appearance and qualities of bread are not changed at all. Christ gives us His Body in a divine and supernatural way, not in a natural way, for His Presence is not natural but Sacramental. The Catholic Doctrine does not suppose such folly of eating Christ's Body in a merely natural sense as we eat ordinary flesh.

An analogy can be found in the manner in which a soul, a spiritual substance, is present in the body. The soul has no dimensions; yet it animates the body which occupies space.

Fr. John Dalgairns explains:

> This then is what God has done to the body of Jesus in the Blessed Sacrament. It has ceased to be extended, and all at once it is freed from the fetters which bound it to a place. It is not so much that it is in many places at once, as that it is no longer under the ordinary laws of space at all. It pervades the Host like a spirit. It uses, indeed, the locality formerly occupied by the bread, in order to fix itself in a definite place, but it only comes into the domain of space at all indirectly through the species, as the soul enters into its present relations with space through the body. Who will say that this involves contradiction, or that it is beyond the power of Omnipotence?

Christ's Teaching

The Jews quarreled among themselves, saying "How can this man give us His flesh to eat?" Jesus said to them, "Amen, amen, I say to you, unless you eat the flesh of the son of man and drink His blood, you do not have life within you" (John 6:52-53).

If Christ did not mean what He said, why would He have turned to the Apostles, to whom He would give the power to change bread and wine into His Flesh and Blood, and say: "Will you also go away?" In other words, "Will you too not believe, and walk away as these who refuse to believe Me?"

Those who heard Christ speak the doctrine of the Real Presence, coupled with the attitude of the Lord, prove the authenticity of the literal meaning. It simply is not possible to interpret these words of Christ in any way except in reference to the actual reception of His holy Body and Blood. The circumstances of the Last Supper give added reason for taking Christ's words literally.

He continued to reaffirm His words which the Jews found so difficult to accept by saying, only moments later: "My Flesh is true Food and my Blood is true Drink" (John 6:56).

Early Witnesses to the Real Presence

Christians from the very beginning believed in the Real Presence of Jesus in the Holy Eucharist, which proves that the belief had to be given by our Lord. Thus St. Paul said:

"The chalice of benediction which we bless, is it not the communion of the Blood of Christ? And the bread which we break, is it not the partaking of the Body of the Lord?"

St. Ignatius of Antioch (d. 117) says: "The Eucharist is the Flesh of our Savior Jesus Christ."

St. Justin Martyr (d.167): "We take this not as ordinary bread nor as ordinary drink, but, as Jesus Christ our Savior."

St. Irenaeus (d. 203): "Wine and bread are by the word of God changed into the Eucharist, which is the Body and Blood of Christ."

St. Hippolytus of Rome (d. 235): "He hath given us His own divine Flesh and His own precious Blood to eat and to drink."

St. Cyril of Jerusalem in the 4th century cautioned his people:

St. Cyril on Communion

> When you approach, do not come with outspread hands and fingers, but make the left hand as it were the throne of the right, which is destined to receive the King, and receive the Body of Christ into the hollow of your hand and say, "Amen." After you have purified your eyes by cautiously applying them to the Sacred Body, be careful, in consuming it, that no particle falls to the ground....Having partaken of the Body of Christ, step forward to take the chalice of the Blood; do not stretch out your hands, but drop them and assuming an attitude

of adoration and homage, say "Amen," and sanctify yourself by participation in the Blood of Christ.

Other Witnesses to Eucharistic Reverence

The Protestant poet and clergyman Lavater, desired to believe in Christ's Real Presence. He once said: "Could I believe that Christ is present in the Blessed Sacrament, I would ever remain on my knees."

Likewise did Prince Hohenloe express himself: "Had I the faith of the Crusader, and were I convinced that Christ is present upon the altar in the monstrance, I could never more leave the Blessed Sacrament all day and would become a monk of the strictest order."

Tertullian offers a classical response: "I believe because it is impossible." And St. Anselm humbly submits his thoughts. "I do not seek to understand in order that I may believe, but believe in order to understand."

Some Christian denominations claim Christ meant He was going to give us a symbol of Himself. Who can conceive of a dying father, having already made out his will leaving a house to a daughter and a business to a son, before he dies presenting a picture of the house to the daughter and a picture of the business to the son saying: "This is what I am leaving you in my last will, a picture of the house and a picture of the business which will always be a symbol, a reminder of me."

Eucharistic Chemistry

A chemistry teacher in a high school claimed the Catholic Church was in error in believing that bread and wine could be changed into the Body and Blood of Jesus as "it is impossible," he said, "to change the nature of a substance."

A Catholic student replied:

> Professor, I am very much surprised to hear you say that bread and wine cannot be changed into flesh and blood. Especially so, to hear you say that in the name of chemistry. What becomes of the bread you eat and the wine you drink? Are they not changed by the laws of nature, of which He is the Author, why can He not effect that change directly and immediately by His own power?

The professor was fair and frank enough to say, "Thanks, I had never before adverted to the fact that the process of metabolism in the human body is constantly effecting much the same change as you believe takes place at the consecration. I withdraw my comment as unfounded and incorrect."

Believing on the Authority of Christ

The mother of a child preparing to make his first Holy Communion asked him: "John, what is it that you are going to receive in Holy Communion?"

"The Body and Blood of Jesus."

"John, it looks like a wafer of bread."

"Yes, it does; but it isn't."

"How do you know it is the Body and Blood of Jesus?"

"Because Jesus said so, and He ought to know!"

The Protestant Revolt

In 1520 Martin Luther attacked the teachings of the Real Presence, as did the Swiss reformer, Huldreich Zwingli. Protestants have to claim Martin Luther, a fallen-away Catholic priest, as their spiritual father, for it was he who taught the world to invent new "doctrines" and to violate Christian unity. What authority did he have to teach this new doctrine? This is not Christ's teaching. To accept Luther's new teaching, or Zwingli's, is to bring alarming attention to St. Paul's warning: "But though we, or an angel from heaven, preach a gospel to you besides that which we have preached to you, let him be anathema" (Gal. 1:8).

Behind the high altar of the Benedictine Church of Ottobeuren in Swabia, Germany, there is a painting representing Christ, whose countenance radiates heavenly calm and divine majesty. On one side of Him is Luther and on the other Zwingli. Beneath the picture is written: "Christ says, this is my Body; Luther says, this will become my body; Zwingli says, this represents my body."

Which of the three is right: Jesus Christ, Martin Luther, or Huldreich Zwingli?

The Council of Trent

The Council of Trent in 1551 replied to the Eucharistic teachings of those in opposition by reaffirming the teachings of the Church from St. Paul in the first century. And in the 6th cannon of the 13th session, the Council said:

> If anyone saith that Christ, the only-begotten Son of God, may not be adored in the Most Blessed Sacrament with the same homage which one owes to God, that one should not venerate Him with particular outward solemnity, that one should not as is the general and widespread custom of the Church, carry Him in solemn procession or expose the Blessed Sacrament to the people for worship, or that those who venerate Him are idolaters, let him be anathema.

Faith and Reason

Faith and reason tell us that Jesus Christ is God; that He taught the doctrine of the Blessed Sacrament as clearly as it is possible to teach it; that Eucharistic worship is unrivaled; and is the characteristic work of the Church Jesus Christ founded; and that the Holy Spirit, the spirit of truth, would not allow the Church to be in error over such a long period of time in such a major doctrine.

The first cell of a baby, magnified sufficiently, resembles a miniature host, and contains the entire person to be. In nine months' time a baby is born. If you reverse the process, instantly, then why is it so difficult to believe Christ can be contained in a host? And break a mirror into a million pieces and see if the sun doesn't shine in each and every particle no matter how minute.

If we had lived two hundred years ago, and if it would be possible to bring a modern automobile, television and an airplane back into that time, what a challenge it would be for us to believe that these were products that came from the earth—that through man's ingenuity they were mined, refined and manufactured! If man, the creature, can place the image of man on two billion television screens throughout the world, and communicate with other men through his voice and actions, then what is so difficult in believing the Creator can do so through Holy Communion, communicating Himself to us. If the creature can produce such marvels, what about the Creator?

Mary: Be It Done According to Thy Word

When Mary was asked to give God a body, her response was: "Be it done unto me according to Thy word" (Lk 1:38). Never doubting that she could conceive while remaining a virgin, she became the first tabernacle and receiving the first Holy Communion by receiving Jesus Christ into her heart, her soul, her womb.

At the wedding feast of Cana she told the servants to "Do whatever He tells you: (John 2:5). The servants obeyed our Lord and filled the six stone jars with water. Christ then performed His first public miracle by changing water into wine. The miracle was profoundly described by the English poet, Richard Crashaw: "When the servants filled the six stone jars with water, the unconscious water looked at its God and blushed." The unconscious water did what conscious man should do in doubting our Lord.

Eucharistic Miracles

In Lanciano, Italy, over twelve hundred years ago, a Consecrated Host bled. Down through the centuries, the townspeople of Lanciano have revered this Host as a continuing miracle attesting to the true presence of our Lord in the Blessed Sacrament. People have come from all over the world to see this Host, which is housed in a special monstrance.

As one would expect, there have been skeptics, especially in modern times. "A Host bleeding?" "Mere tradition, just tradition," the skeptics said.

Scientific Tests In 1970 the Holy See ordered a thorough scientific investigation using spectroscopic analysis, high powered microscopes and advanced medical technology. The most illustrious scientist, Professor Odoardo Linoli, eminent professor in anatomy and pathological histology as well as in chemistry and clinical microscopy, headed the investigation and was assisted by Professor Ruggero Bertellie of the University of Siena. The investigation showed the Host had turned into flesh, into a very fine slice of human heart, and was incorrupt, as though it had just been taken from a heart.

The analyses were conducted with unquestionable scientific precision and were documented with a series of photographs which were made public by Professor Linoli on March 4, 1971 in the church of the miracle.

More Tests Other scientists were asked by the Holy See to verify these findings. When all of the data was accumulated, the scientists were in accord: "Without reservation, this is a slice of tissue from a human heart, as though it had been expertly excised by a surgeon's scalpel through the center of the heart. And, though subject to disintegration as all flesh is, it remains incorrupt." These findings were published in September of 1971 in the official newspaper of the Vatican, *L'Osservatore Romano.*

Catholic publications carried the story of the investigation and its findings; but, generally speaking, little attention was given in the secular press. Such is the way the world receives miracles. Yet, could any scientific discovery be more meaningful or extraordinary?

Because of this miracle, Lanciano was chosen as the site for the First Eucharistic Congress for the region of Abruzzi, Italy, which was held on September 23-25, 1921.

Healing Power of the Eucharist

Fr. Aloysius Ellacuria, C.M.F., founder of the Missionaries of Perpetual Adoration, had a young mother come to him in the early 1970's, eyes filled with tears, an aching body saturated with cancer, and given little time to live. He took her into the chapel asking her, "Have you ever asked our Lord to cure you?" "No," she replied. "Well," he said, "Let us kneel down right here in front of the Blessed Sacrament, and let us ask Him to cure you." "You know Our Lord is present in the Blessed Sacrament; do you believe that?" "Yes," she promptly replied. Father continued, "Our Lord is the same as He who walked on this earth 2,000 years ago; and who blessed the sick and healed the sick. Do you believe that He is the same Lord that is here living in the Blessed Sacrament?" "Yes, He is," was her pain filled response. "Well, He cured them and He can cure you." Together they prayed a series of

"Our Father's, Hail Mary's and Glory Be's." After three of each the woman, startled, said: "Father, I don't think it is necessary to go on—I feel healed!"

X rays were taken the next day and the doctor, astonished, said: "All the cells that were attacked by the cancer are now the cells of a new-born baby."

This was but one of many cures Fr. Aloysius was responsible for while in the presence of the Blessed Sacrament imploring our Lord for assistance.

Miracles Today

Fr. Angelo Caserta, pastor of St. Boniface Church in Piqua, Ohio, wrote the following article in his June 10, 1990 Sunday church bulletin:

> I don't recall the exact time when this happened but that does not really matter. Some two months ago or more someone had received Holy Communion and then took the Sacred Host out of his/her mouth, leaving it in the church pew. Annie Koenig was cleaning up the church when she noticed the host and brought it to her mother, Carol, who gave it to me. Someone had definitely placed it in his/her mouth. I took the Sacred Host to the sacristy, put water in a small glass container and then broke up the Sacred Host into small pieces so that it would disintegrate. I placed it on the far end of the counter but shortly forgot about it.

On May 25th when I was putting things in order I noticed the glass container had something in it. When I had it to the rectory to clean it I noticed that there were blood stains on the glass. Upon examining it I saw where there was a great deal of blood, and not just a faint sprinkling of it. *I know with certainty that it is the precious blood of Jesus.* There is no other explanation. Jesus let this all happen and while I do not know the reason, yet I am also sure that He had something definite in mind....

When this happened it brought to my mind Sister Donatiana, our long-time first and second grade teacher, so admired by every one of us. I recall how at the strike of the church clock on the hour we folded our hands and then prayed: "Eternal Father, I offer Thee the wounds of our Lord Jesus Christ to heal the wounds of my soul." And "O Jesus, pardon and mercy through the merits of Your sacred wounds." You will also remember how many times in speaking of the Real Presence of Jesus in the most Blessed Sacrament we would recite that Jesus is present in the Holy Eucharist as God and Man, with Body and Soul, with Flesh and Blood, in His Divinity and with His Humanity. And He is!

I remember too reciting in the second grade: Praised and adored be without end, Jesus in the most Blessed Sacrament. How can we ever thank God for the gift of His Son, and His Son for the gift of Himself in the Holy Eucharist?

The Witness of the Devil

A celebrated Jesuit, Fr. Deliro, relates the following incident: in 1617, a woman living in Cambrai, France, was possessed by the devil. The dean of Cambrai, a pious and learned priest, made use of the exorcisms of the Church, but for a long time met with no success; the devil scoffed at all his efforts. One day the priest went to the possessed person immediately after Mass, in order to begin a new exorcism. The devil cried out to him from afar: "Thou art very strong today on account of the bread which thou has eaten at the altar."

"No quibbling or evasions," answered the priest. "If what I have eaten today in Holy Communion is but common bread, then my voice shall be without power and authority against thee, but if, as I believe with my whole soul, it is the Body of our Lord Jesus Christ, then I command thee in His name to leave the woman instantly." At the same moment the devil uttered a frightful cry and left the woman, to return no more.

In Laon, France, in 1566, the devil showed his faith in the Blessed Sacrament and his dread thereof witnessed by more than 150,000 persons many of whom were Protestants who would be converted to the Catholic Faith.

A Case Involving Pope St. Pius V

By order of Pope Saint Pius V, Fr. John de Boulese drew up a special document relating the facts. A woman, Nicola Pierrot, was possessed by the devil in such a manner that she suddenly became horribly distorted. The exorcisms only served to ascertain that she was possessed by the prince of devils, Beelzebub. She could not be freed from his power. At length the bishop approached her with the Sacred Host, whereupon the devil uttered a horrible bellowing which made all shutter. The evil spirit left the woman repeatedly, but returned as soon as the Sacred Host was removed. Repeatedly he withdrew amid fearful howling, writhing and struggling as soon as the Sacred Host was again brought near. Being commanded by the bishop, the demon furiously confessed: "I acknowledge that here is truly the Son of God. He is my Lord. It pains me to confess it, but I am compelled to do so; yes, I will be obliged through the power of this Body to depart from hence." And the devil finally did depart, to return no more, at three o'clock in the afternoon on a Friday, the day and the hour when our Lord triumphed over hell and Satan on the cross. The woman was perfectly cured.

Stealing the Body of the Lord

Jonathan of Enghein (Hainut), Belgium, a rich Jewish banker, bribed John of Louvain, a supposed convert to Catholicism, to bring him some Consecrated Hosts. The robber stole the ciborium containing the Hosts from St. Catherine's Church, on the outskirts of Brussels. The Jew had them in his house but a few days, when, while walking in his garden, he was rushed upon and murdered. His widow cried: "This is the vengeance of the God of the Christians. I could not bear to have that (the ciborium of Hosts) any longer in my house."

The Hosts were then handed over to Jews in Brussels who awaited Good Friday (April 30, 1370) for the exhibition of their devilish hatred. They scattered the Sacred Hosts on the table and pierced Them with knives; when, to their great amazement, Blood came form the Sacred Hosts. Like their ancestors in the Garden of Olives, they fell over, as if struck to the ground. With great fear, and wanting to get rid of the Hosts, they asked a woman named Catherine, another false convert to Catholicism, to take them to Cologne.

Overcome by remorse, Catherine reported the fact to the pastor of Our Lady Chapel, and repeated her accusation before witnesses. The leaders of the Synagogue were arrested. Proven guilty, they confessed their crime and were punished according to the code of those days.

Of the sixteen miraculous Hosts, three have been and are still preserved in the Church of St. Gudule, in an elegant montrance which is carried in procession annually through the streets of the city. Others were placed in a chapel erected in their honor and called "The Chapel of the Blessed Sacrament of the Miracle." The scenes of this sacrilege are portrayed in white stone, embedded in the blue flags on the floor; they are also embroidered on rich gold cloth, hung up around the walls of the sacred edifice.

St. Anthony and the Mule of Bovillus

Known as the patron saint of lost articles, St. Anthony of Padua helped an obstinate heretic named Bovillus of Tolosa, Spain, find our Lord in the Blessed Sacrament. Bovillus denied the presence upon being confronted by St. Anthony. However, he said he would believe if he could see a miracle in proof of it. "What, then, do you desire?" asked St. Anthony. "I will keep my mule without food for three days," said Bovillus, "then I will bring him to you. On one side I will place food before him, and on the other side you shall stand with the Blessed Sacrament. In case the mule leaves the food and goes to you, I will believe that Jesus Christ is truly and really present in the Blessed Sacrament."

St. Anthony agreed to the proposal. On the day appointed a great gathering of people were assembled in the public square to see the issue. St. Anthony, after having said Mass, took the Blessed Sacrament and carried It with him to the square. Then, when the hungry animal had been brought near and food put before him, St. Anthony, holding the Blessed Sacrament in his hands, spoke: "In the name of my Creator, Whom I am not worthy to hold in my hands, I command thee to draw near and prostrate thyself before thy God, to give due honor to Him, that the heretics may learn from thee how they ought to worship their God in the Blessed Sacrament."

As soon as St. Anthony spoke the words, the mule left his food, went before the Blessed Sacrament, and bowed his head to the ground as if to adore It. At this sight, Bovillus, and many other heretics were converted and professed their faith in the Real Presence.

St. John Vianney and the Protestants

"One day," said St. John Vianney, "two Protestant ministers came to me who did not believe in the Real Presence of our Lord in the the Blessed Sacrament."

> I said to them: "Do you think a piece of bread could detach itself, and of its own accord, go and place itself on the tongue of a person who came near to receive it?" "No," they said. "Well, then it is not bread."
>
> There was a man who had doubts about the Real Presence, and he said: "What do we know about it? It is not certain what consecration is! What happens on the altar at that moment?" But this man

> wished to believe, and he prayed to the Blessed Virgin to obtain faith for him. Listen attentively to this: I do not say that this happened somewhere, but I say that it happened to myself. At the moment when this man came up to receive Holy Communion the Sacred Host detached Itself from my fingers, while I was yet a good way off, went of Itself and placed Itself upon the tongue of that man.

Universal Early Christian Faith in the Eucharist

In every country, for the first eight hundred years, no one publicly doubted Christ's actual presence in the Holy Eucharist. In the year 844 the first systematic treatise on the Holy Eucharist was published by Paschasius Radbertus of Corbie (near Amiens, France), entitled *On the Body and Blood of the Lord,* which triggered the first conflict. In a work carrying the same title, Ratramnus, a monk, also of Corbie, regarded the Eucharist as merely a memorial. Other writers of the period took part in the controversy. Hincmar, Remigius of Rheims, and Ratherius of Verona, siding with Paschasius, and Amalarius of Metz, Florus of Lyons, and Rabanus Maurus, taking the opposition.

And Conflict Only Later

Two centuries elapsed before the conflict was again discussed. Fuel fired the controversy when Berengarius of Tours attacked the real presence. Transubstantiation, he held, "was contrary to reason, unwarranted by Scripture, and inconsistent with the teaching of men like Ambrose, Jerome and Augustine." He did not conceal his conviction from his scholars and friends, and through them the report spread widely that he denied the common doctrine of Christ's actual presence in the Holy Eucharist. After he was refuted by Bishop Hugo of Langres, he still held firm his belief and was eventually excommunicated by Pope Leo IX. Berengarius continued in his obstinacy with the additional logic, "If Christ is in heaven, as the Scriptures say, He cannot be on earth or on many altars, since nobody can be in different places at the same time."

Differing Liturgical Customs

Up until the 11th century, out of great respect for the hidden God in the Eucharist, the consecrated host and chalice were never elevated during the Holy Sacrifice of the Mass. The only time the consecrated Host was displayed was at communion. The elevating of the host and chalice originated in this century as did the ringing of the bell announcing the moment of consecration. The elevation was not introduced as a protest against Berengarius' false doctrine, however, it was, "...an eloquent liturgical gesture indicating that the bread is truly and actually changed into the Body of the Lord and must necessarily be venerated. It was a summons to worship."

While the consecrated Host was elevated, everyone was encouraged to say "My Lord and my God!" At the elevation of the precious Blood, various prayers were in vogue, one of which was "Jesus, by Your precious Blood, purify my heart and my soul."

The Feast of Corpus Christi

In 1264, Pope Urban IV, instituted the feast of Corpus Christi (Body of Christ) "...to compensate for the lack of reverence exhibited daily at the celebration of the Holy Mass and for transgressions committed through negligence." The energetic repudiation of Berengarius' false doctrine created an attitude of mind which encouraged and prepared the way for greater attention to the adoration of Jesus in the Blessed Sacrament.

Henry VIII & St. Thomas More

Henry VIII abandoned the Catholic Church in 1534, making himself the head of the Church of England, and so thinking to ensure the stability of the English monarchy. But when King Henry VIII's Lord Chancellor, St. Thomas More, was confronted by his friends for his frequent communion, which they said took away much of his valuable time for other matters, he replied:

> Your reasons for wanting me to stay away from Holy Communion are exactly the ones which cause me to go so often. My distractions are great, but it is in Communion that I recollect myself. I have temptations many times a day. By daily Holy Communion I get the strength to overcome them. I have very much important business to handle; I need light and wisdom. It is for these very reasons that I go to Holy Communion every day to consult Jesus about them.

And all the more he would pray "Give me the grace to long for Your holy Sacraments, and especially to rejoice in the presence of Your Body, sweet Savior Christ, in the Holy Sacrament of the altar."

7.
Adoration and Reparation

The Apparitions at Knock

One of the great apparitions of our Lady was in the Irish village of Knock. On August 21, 1879, surrounded by light, wearing a brilliant golden crown, and long white cloak, she appeared. On her right appeared St. Joseph inclining reverently towards her; on her left St. John the Evangelist, attired as a bishop and holding a book, his hand raised as if preaching. To St. John's left was an altar on which stood a lamb, surrounded by angels' wings, a symbol of the Holy Sacrifice of the Mass. This wondrous spectacle lasted two hours in the rain. No word was spoken to the fifteen persons of different ages, occupations and intelligence who knelt while witnessing the apparition. Since nothing was spoken, it was to become known as "The Silent Apparition," to bring to our attention the importance of the Holy Sacrifice of the Mass, and that Christ is truly present in the Blessed Sacrament which we should venerate in silence, awe and reverence.

Wherever approved apparitions of our Blessed Lady have taken place, churches or chapels have been erected in order that the Holy Sacrifice of the Mass may be offered for the greater honor and glory of God, and as places to keep the Blessed Sacrament.

St. Catherine Labouré

Our Blessed Lady said to St. Catherine Labouré "Come to the foot of the altar. Here graces will be poured out upon all who ask them with confidence and fervor. They will be bestowed upon the great and upon the small."

She spoke these encouraging words on July 18, 1830. She came to Catherine again on November 27th, holding a globe with a tiny cross on top. She held it out as if offering it to God. Rays of light streamed down from some of the gems on her fingers. Lowering her eyes, she said to Catherine, "This ball you see is the world. I am praying for it and for everyone in the world. The rays are the graces which I give to those who ask for them. But there are no rays from some of these stones, for many people do not receive graces because they do not ask for them."

Upon such encouragement from our Lady, with what awe and unspeakable gratitude should we not kneel in solemn stillness before the Blessed Sacrament, this fountain of grace. We can immerse our hearts and souls in an ocean of peace and blessedness in making acts of adoration, love, thanksgiving, atonement and petition.

As the sun sends out its rays, giving light, heat and life, so too from the Real Presence of Jesus in the Blessed Sacrament come forth the rays of divine grace, bringing light where there was darkness, heat where all was cold, life where before was death.

St. Margaret Mary Alacoque

To St. Margaret Mary, Jesus said: "Behold this Heart which has so loved men that it spared nothing, even going so far as to exhaust and consume itself, to prove to them its love. And in return I receive from the greater part of men nothing but ingratitude, by the contempt, irreverence, sacrileges, and coldness with which they treat me in the Sacrament of Love."

Century has followed century, generation has followed generation, man has become absorbed in science and reason which has rapidly introduced the "Industrial Revolution," the "Electronic Age," and the "Space Age," ignoring our Lord all the more. New discoveries are being made and each one seems to thrust Our Lord farther into the background. Books attacking religion are rolling off of the presses in greater numbers and greater demand. The world as a whole continues to pursue its goals of wealth, power, fame, pleasure. The Church has less to fear, however, from her enemies than from the indifferences of so many Catholics due to their impiety.

Callous ingratitude, continued contempt, irreverence, sacrileges mixed with satanism, and intensified coldness of heart is the reply to our Lord.

Fatima and the Ingratitude of the Modern World

Unabashed our Lord would summon His mother to champion His plea. She in turn would prepare the ground work with an angel sent to three peasant children who had been taught to reverence Jesus in the Blessed Sacrament with this prayer: "Praised be the ever Holy Sacrament of the Eucharist, blessed fruit of the most pure Virgin Mary."

The Angel appeared in the spring of 1916 to these children: Jacinta, Lucia and Francisco, in Fatima, Portugal. Kneeling upon the ground he taught them to pray this prayer which he prayed three times: "My God, I believe, I adore, I hope, and I love You. Forgive those who do not believe, do not adore, do not hope, and do not love You."

The Golden Chalice

The last time the angel would come would be the fall of that year. He would hold a golden chalice in his hand and above it a Host from which drops of Blood were falling into the chalice. Leaving both suspended in the air, prostrating himself upon the ground, he taught the children to pray this prayer which again he prayed three times:

> Most Holy Trinity, Father, Son and Holy Ghost, I adore You profoundly. I offer You the most precious Body, Blood, Soul and Divinity of Jesus Christ, present in all the tabernacles of the world, in reparation for the outrages, sacrileges, and indifferences by which He is offended. Through the infinite merits of the Sacred Heart of Jesus and the Immaculate Heart of Mary, I beg you for the conversion of sinners.

Afterwards, he rose and took again the chalice and the Host and gave the Host to Lucia and the contents of the chalice to Jacinta and Francisco to drink, saying at the same time: "Receive the Body and Blood of Jesus Christ, so horribly outraged by ungrateful men. Console your God and make reparation."

On the Feast of Our Lady of the Blessed Sacrament

The stage was dramatically set for the Lady to make her presence known! Was it a coincidence, or was it to reiterate Her Son's plea, that she chose May 13, 1917, to come to the children? May 13th is the feast day of Our Lady of the Blessed Sacrament....

Bathed in light coming from the apparition, the children were astonished at her beauty. Here is Lucia's description: "It was a lady, clothed in white, brighter than the sun, radiating a light more clear and intense than a crystal cup filled with sparkling water, pierced by burning sunlight." She asked the children "Will you offer yourselves to God, and bear all the sufferings which He sends you, in reparation for the sins which offend Him, and in supplication for the conversion of sinners?" How could they refuse her? She is the spiritual mother of all mankind, and who can say "no" to a mother? Promptly the children answered "Yes, we will."

The Need for Eucharistic Reparation

She came to them in her last of six apparitions on Oct. 13, 1917, with an air of sadness telling them: "People must offend our Lord no more, and they must ask pardon for their sins, for He is already too much offended."

Nothing shows the decay of piety and the loss of all sense of religion among Christians as does the disrespectful behavior in the house of God. An unrestrained love of the world has blinded us so that we follow its customs to an unhealthy love of ease, and unbridled love of pleasure, and egotistical sense of praise, and a desire for diversions which have contributed to a loss of the sacred.

By contrast, silence and an exterior respect in posture should accompany us into our churches as we present ourselves and pay homage to Jesus in the Blessed Sacrament. "In whose presence the highest seraphim annihilate themselves," said St. Ludger, Bishop of Munster, "we must observe silence not only with our tongues, but also with our bodies out of respect to the presence of God on the altar, and also not to give the least occasion of distraction to others." To make reparation and adore Our Lord, we should strive to be dead to all creatures and close our senses to every object that can distract our minds from God.

8.
Glittering Bubbles and Itching Ears

Ever since man lost God's friendship, he has sought to regain it. When born, a baby comes into the world with fists clenched, symbolic of wanting to regain what was lost. Where before the fall it was necessary to hang on, now it is important to let go to have that union. In death our hands are open to symbolize letting go. Just as it was vital not to eat the forbidden fruit to gain eternal life, now the reverse is true; we must eat the Bread of Life, the Holy Eucharist, to gain eternal life.

The Way of the World and the Way of Christ

What the forbidden fruit was to Adam and Eve, the glittering bubbles of the world are to us; empty and vain. Like charm, they are deceptive; like beauty, they are fleeting. In our society, money, pleasure and power are considered everything. The wisdom of God is foolishness to the world just as the wisdom of the world is foolishness to God. The world says "Eat, drink, be merry." Christ says "Deny yourself."

The Case of Oscar Wilde

One of the famous cemeteries in Paris is Pere La Chaise. There lies buried Oscar Wilde, poet, playwright, and orator who wrote and spoke our language with a brilliance and an eloquence which has rarely been surpassed. He was the symbol of refinement, learning, and culture, and became one of the most prominent personalities of his day. His witty sayings were quoted on both sides of the Atlantic. His rooms were decorated with peacock feathers, lilies, sunflowers and expensive blue china. The picture of Dorian Gray was the mirror of his life. Yet he fell to the lowest depths of degradation and fled in shame and disgrace to seek refuge in the soil of France, changing his name to Sebastion Melmoth.

Born in Dublin on October 15, 1856, his soul was required by God on November 30, 1900, having been allotted forty-four years to prepare for eternity. He squandered his Catholic life, preferring forbidden fruits and the pleasures of the moment to the Bread of life and the joys of eternity.

The following is taken from the April 9, 1990 issue of *People Magazine* and speaks for itself:

> He had talent...he had style...he had energy...he lived so fast that his first and last names blew off in prop-wash...he traveled with the international jet set...he was one of the first superstars of fashion...he died of AIDS...It is a cruel irony that the pain and ugliness of the disease that the 'Great Halston' died from has bored to the heart of an industry committed to the image of perfection and beauty.

To add to the irony, the Chicago Tribune carried his once handsome picture with an article singing his praises in the edition of April 1st—April Fool's Day.

Worldy Amusements

Viewed in the eyes of the saints, how insignificant and contemptible do the idle amusements of the great ones of the world appear! How trifling that uninterrupted succession of serious folly or empty pleasures which engages the greatest part of mankind. After all their turmoils they find their hands empty, and feel their hearts filled only with fears, remorse, and bitterness, instead of holy peace and joy, with the riches of eternity.

St. Cyril of Alexandria

How frail we are, placed in a world that would blind us, swallow us up, dangling its fascinating wares before our searching eyes. In contrast, we ought to follow the admonition of St. Cyril of Alexandria:

If the poison of pride is swelling up in you, turn to the Eucharist; and that Bread, Which is your God humbling and disguising Himself, will teach you humility. If the fever of selfish greed rages in you, feed on the Bread; and you will learn generosity. If the cold wind of coveting withers you, hasten to the Bread of Angels; and charity will come to blossom in your heart. If you feel the itch of intemperance, nourish yourself with the Flesh and Blood of Christ, Who practiced heroic self-control during His earthly life; and you will become temperate. If you are lazy and sluggish about spiritual things, strengthen yourself with the heavenly Food; and you will grow fervent. Lastly, if you feel scorched by the fever of impurity, go to the banquet of the Angels; and the spotless Flesh of Christ will make you pure and chaste.

Holy Communion to Combat Sin

Receiving Jesus in Holy Communion makes us conscious of His love, deepens our reality of God, realizing too that He is a witness to our every deed, the auditor of our every word, the spectator of our thoughts and aspirations, and it helps us to realize that the greatest realities of life are those which are spiritual and lie beyond the reach of the senses of man.

Spiritual writers have always counseled people aspiring to sanctity to empty themselves as much as possible, especially of created things, and become a vacuum thirsting to be filled with God. If the heart is dissipated among many concerns, sufficient attention will not be given to the Divine Guest about to enter the chambers of our heart. We can become casual if we don't display genuine reverence for the Holy Eucharist. Our wills are free to harmonize or refuse to harmonize with the will of God by the acceptance or the refusal of His supreme gifts. He forces His will on no one.

Caryll Houselander

The twentieth century English mystic, Caryll Houselander, in her book *The Reed of God,* wrote of our blessed Lady, "God looked over the world for an empty heart—a heart that was empty like a flute on which He could pipe a tune...and the emptiest heart He could find was the heart of a lady. Since there was no self there, He filled it with His Very Self." And, because of this, Mary became to God what the moon is to the sun, a perfect reflection shining like a beacon in a world darkened by sin.

Unlike Mary who went to God "full of grace," we go as sinners. But God does not demand a pure heart before embracing us, nor does He look at our sins, guilt, or shame. All He wants us to do is to turn away from sin and be honest with Him. Ever since Adam's first sin, man has been in the business of camouflage trying to hide his sins from God. Because honesty is conformity to God's will, and the ultimate goal of complete honesty is union with God, Alexander Pope would say: "An honest man is the noblest work of God."

Turning Back to God

God pours forth such tremendous graces upon the soul that turns from her erring ways and unites her will to God's that the Venerable Blosius said: "He, who at the moment of death, makes an act of perfect conformity to the Divine Will, shall be delivered not only from hell, but also from purgatory, though he had been guilty of all the sins of the world."

In the last minute of his life the good thief did just that, turned from his sin to conformity to the Divine Will, and he was given heaven: "Amen I say to thee this day thou shalt be with Me in paradise" (Luke 23:43).

And it is not the only case where a soul stole heaven in the last moment of his life. St. Mary Magdalen de Pazzi who told Cardinal Medici that he would become a Pope (he became Pope Leo XI), prayed for two evildoers who were being hung for their deeds. They repented, one so much so that in a vision she saw his soul "take flight into paradise," for his heart was filled with honest sorrow and resignation to his plight.

A God Touched By Honesty

Even earthly kings are touched by honesty and have rewarded it. When Frederick II inspected a Berlin prison in the eighteenth century, he was beset on all sides by prisoners protesting their innocence. However, one prisoner remained off in a corner, seemingly unconcerned. Puzzled, Frederick asked him, "Why are you here?"

"Armed robbery," was the reply. "Were you guilty?" the king wanted to know. "Oh, yes," the prisoner replied, " and I deserve to be punished."

Calling the warden, Frederick ordered him to release the man. "I will not have him kept in this prison where he will corrupt all the innocent people who occupy it," he said.

A Battle with Powers and Principalities

Wandering through the many snares of life, Satan, with all his cunning, never ceases to seek to enslave the human appetites, imagination, and senses, so that one becomes more interested in self-gratification than in what our God-given conscience dictates.

Indeed, we live in the times that St. Paul warned about: "For the time will come when people will not tolerate sound doctrine, but, following their own desires, they will surround themselves with teachers who tickle their ears. They will stop listening to the truth and will wander off to fables" (2 Tim. 4:3-4).

Marketing God?

In the Sunday edition of April 13-15, 1990, the *Detroit News* enclosed a special section on religion offering five pages that began with the caption: "Gimme that New-Time Religion." The front page carried a picture of Pastor Bill Hybels who heads the Willow Creek Community Church in South Barrington, Illinois, and offers a

> slick, show-biz service where drama and soft rock are served up on a stage washed in pink and blue spotlights. A soft-sell sermon is delivered by Hybels from a lucite lectern.... It's been put down as pop Gospel, fast food theology, McChurch...where you won't be bored...Drama, humor and pop music...14,500 show up every Sunday...no altar, no robes, no stained glass windows...complete with 12 big screen TVs showing close-up action onstage, just like the rock concerts.

The article goes on to say that "to attract churchgoers today, you've got to please the customer. That means high-tech entertainment by professionals: actors, singers, etc. No Bible-thumping."

It continues: "At Trinity Episcopal Cathedral in Sacramento, California, a warm, personal welcome—and comfort food—are doing the trick. On Monday evenings, each Sunday visitor to Trinity receives a knock at the door from a church member with a pie in hand and ready to discuss what the church offers."

"In 1989, we delivered 154 pies, and we had about 98 persons join who had received pies," says James Snell, clergy director of the program. David Affleck said the pie helped him choose the congregation. Upon receiving his pie he said "Wow! That's nice!"

How-To Seminars Instead of Prayer

Pastor Hybels' success has other pastors lining up for thrice-yearly "how-to" seminars. Even churches disdainful of Willow Creek are hustling to add punch to their pitch—from home-baked pies to high-tech telemarketing to day-care.

The approach is as old as Adam and Eve, who accepted the first apple "pie-in-the-sky." Christ did not give us a church to move with the world, but a Church which will move the world.

Food that Perishes

Satan diverts from the truth. Recall to mind Christ's words: "Do not labor for the food that perishes, but for that which endures unto life everlasting which the Son of Man will give" (John 6:27). And from the beginning of Protestantism in the year 1517, of the millions of Protestant ministers, where is even one to be found who has been able to do what every Catholic priest has been doing from the year 33 until today: give us the Bread "which endures unto life everlasting" by changing bread and wine into the Body and Blood of Christ?

St. Vincent of Lerins on Novelty and Heresy

St. Vincent of Lerins maintained that all novelty in faith is a certain mark of heresy; and in religion nothing is more to be dreaded than ears itching after new teachers. He said: "They who have made bold with one article of faith will proceed on to others; and what will be the consequence of this religion but only that these refiners will never have done enough until they have reformed it away." He added that heretics are like those poisoners or quacks who mask their destructive potions under the names of good drugs and infallible cures. They imitate the father of lies, who quoted scripture against the Son of God when he tempted Him.

The Church: Mainstay of Truth

Living in a world of distracting thoughts and tumult, pestered with numberless heresies, has caused much grief. Confusion is rampant. Many Catholics are straying into Fundamentalist churches where the big emphasis is the Bible and not the church. The Bible, clipped, misread and misquoted is a powerful instrument in their hands. It is used as a source of private inspiration without any authoritative guiding power. Such Christians maintain that the pillar and mainstay of truth is the Bible, yet the Bible itself says that the church, not the Bible, is the "pillar and mainstay of truth" (1 Tim. 3:15). All such churches offer the menu without the meal. The Catholic Church offers the menu—the Bible—and the meal—the Holy Eucharist!

If one decides to leave Christ and His Catholic Church, because of finding that the doctrine is too difficult and the moral teaching too challenging, one is prone to accept any false teaching. Remember the parable of the prodigal son. He had all he wanted and more, but ended up considering acorns a luxury, actually envying the pigs who could fill their bellies on them....Leave Christ and His Church and you will be left with acorns.

Satanists Hate the Eucharist

The ex-Satan worshiper Betty Brennan, in speaking to a Pentecostal prayer group, gives us a different sort of testimony to the importance of Christ in the Eucharist:

> For years, for years, I have persecuted the church. When I left and went back to the church, I picked the Roman Catholic Church because every Satanic ritual is a take-off on the Roman Catholic Sacraments. They (satanists) know what the Eucharist is...if everybody here, and everybody that came into the renewal, understood the Sacrament of the Eucharist—the Word enfleshed—they would not end up in a Pentecostal Church with a relationship with a book—how can you leave a

Sacramental church and go to another denomination following a word, a book? The word of Jesus Christ brings you to the Word enfleshed, the Eucharist!

Do you know that if there was a bona fide witch here and you put out thirty hosts, or a thousand hosts, and only one was consecrated, they would know immediately which one was consecrated—because of the presence! And yet we will go to x amount of conferences, x amount of prayer meetings, x amount of time with our prayer partner, but we don't have that desire to be one with the Body, Blood, Soul and Divinity of Jesus Christ Himself!

The Prophetic Writings of St. Vincent of Lerins

Again, St. Vincent of Lerins had a remarkable foresight and could have been writing for troubled souls today who have defected from the true faith of Catholicism, abandoning the Eucharist and therefore the Presence of Christ. "Souls which have lost the anchorage of the Catholic Faith," he said,

> are tossed and shattered with inward storms of clashing thoughts, that by this restless posture of mind they may be made sensible of their danger; and taking down the sails of pride and vanity, which they have unhappily spread before every gust of heresy, they may make all the sail they can into the safe and peaceful harbor of their holy mother the Catholic Church; and being

sick from an excess of errors may there discharge those foul and bitter waters to make room for the pure water of life. There they may unlearn well what they have learned ill; may get a right notion of all those doctrines of the church they are capable of understanding, and believe those that surpass all understanding.

9. Hope of Our Times

We live in an extraordinary age, an age of amazing development and rapid advance in all that concerns material progress, which could not have been foreseen, and would not have been believed possible had it been foretold in the beginning of this century.

With all of the undeniable good that has been accomplished, a mood of selfishness, love of pleasure, and refusal to discipline ourselves has caused us to lose control of our rational thoughts as more and more we look for instant bodily gratifications. We want to be saved from poverty, war, disease and economic insecurity but we do not want to be freed from our passions.

The Way of the World

Our Lord looks about the world for people of honor, unassuming, like the Apostle Nathaniel, who delighted our Lord, and of whom He said, "Behold, a true Israelite in whom there is no guile" (John 1:47). But we are bent on going in other directions, like the impetuous Peter who denied Him, not once, but three times: "I do not know the Man" (John 18:17, 25, 27); like Thomas, who said, "Unless I see in His hands the print of the nails, and put my finger into the place of the nails, and put my hand into His side, I will not believe" (John 21:25); like James and John, who conspired with their mother to ask Jesus for first place: "Command that these my two sons may sit, one at Thy right hand and one at Thy left hand, in Thy kingdom" (Matt. 20:21); or even like Judas, who exchanged his Lord for 30 pieces of silver: "What are you willing to give me for delivering Him to you?" (Matt. 26:15).

Pride and Defiance

And our generation tends, more and more to look up to God, not out of adoration, love, awe, and thanksgiving, but in defiance "Come down from the Cross and we will believe." Instead of bowing down to God, we expect Him to bow down to us. We have lost the humility that kept the child in us alive. "We have grown too proud," said Abraham Lincoln, "to acknowledge the God Who made us."

All the evils of the times stem from our abandonment of Christ. The fire of love is the Real Presence of Christ in the Holy Eucharist has to be more and more kindled in the hearts of men, and the most Blessed Sacrament has to be recognized as the bond of peace, unity, and reconciliation for all nations.

Keeping God's Commandments

King David recognized that peace and unity could only be attained if we "keep the charge of the Lord thy God, to walk in His ways, to keep His statutes, and His Commandments, and His judgments, and His testimonies, as it is written in the law of Moses" (1 Kings 1:2).

Spiritual Battle

The world is a great battle-field on which two hostile spirits are contending for the mastery, not only of this world, but of every human soul: "The life of man upon earth," said the holy Job, "is a warfare." Every soul is subject to the action of these two spirits and belongs to one or the other contending camp.

No one is, or can be, neutral in this war, for "No one can serve two masters; for either he will hate the one and love the other, or he will hold to the one and despise the other" (Matt. 6:24). We may be on one side today and on the other tomorrow; but we can never say, at any one instant of our life, that we are between the two and that we belong neither to God nor Satan. What is particularly startling in this warfare is the fact that our eternal destiny depends upon the side on which we shall be found when death shall end the combat for each one of us. If we fall fighting for God, having loved

Him and our neighbor, our lot shall be with the princes of the kingdom; if we fall in the ranks of Satan, under the standard of the world and its principles, we shall share the fate of those who sided with Lucifer, the leader of rebellion, and our cause is lost for all eternity.

The Great Trials of the Church

The present trials of the Church, and of countries, is greater than any other period previously. The presence and the power of God are never wanting to His Church, but it is in the hour of danger when the Church is most fiercely attacked and when the enemies of God have put forth their united strength and their cunning to ensnare the children of God, that this divine guidance and protection are manifested.

Adolf Hitler and the Triumph of Evil

In the main street of the little Austrian border town of Braunau-am-Inn, facing Bavaria across the river, stands a modest dwelling. Here, on April 20, 1889, Adolf Hitler was born. Some mystics have said that he was one of the three anti-Christs, the first being Napoleon. However that may be, it is doubtful that any man in the history of the world has ever wielded such authority, power, and influence; was so loved; or had such hypnotic powers to strike fear into so many people, as he did.

Forty-five years after he was born, Herman Goering was to say: “We love Adolf

Hitler because we believe deeply and unswervingly that God has sent Him to us to save Germany." And again Herman Goering, after the "Blood purge" of June 1934:

> Der Fuehrer accomplishes great deeds out of the greatness of his heart, the passion of his will, and the goodness of his soul. We are all the creatures of Der Fuehrer. His faith makes us the most powerful of men. If he removes his confidence, we are nothing, we are plunged into darkness and lost to the memory of man. For Germany is Adolph Hitler.

And thus Hans Franck, with the fervent approval of his countrymen, would say: "Hitler is like God!"

Hitler usurped with satanic delight the honor and glory that only Jesus deserves. The ultimate judgement of mankind on this man and his work is perhaps better reflected in the comments of his contemporaries. Joseph Stalin, speaking on the 25th anniversary of the Russian Revolution, described Hitler as a "cannibal." Neville Chamberlain, on the day of his resignation as Prime Minister of England said: "In all history no other man has been responsible for such a hideous total of human suffering and misery as he." Winston Churchill called him "a monster of wickedness, insatiable in his lust for blood and plunder." Hitler used the fanaticism of his followers to spread agony and grief over the earth.

Hitler may represent for us the extent to which the modern era has given itself to evil, especially as so many of the evils he practiced are becoming commonplace again today, particularly that of abortion.

> Whether Hitler's ghost will walk again, whether contemporary civilization will breed new Hitlerisms, depends upon men's capacity to render their collective lives in a fashion promising hope and self-fulfillment rather than misery, frustration and madness. In this sense, Adolph Hitler will remain a challenge to the world society of the atomic age.*

The Eucharistic Alternative

Although we live in turbulent and uncertain times, we are also living in the age of the Eucharist. Dwelling on our altars and in the tabernacles is the Lord Jesus Christ, to comfort and sustain those who turn to Him. He will, in His own good time, dispel the clouds of war and restore peace, for He alone is "The Way, the Truth and the Life," not only of individual souls but also of nations.

Devotion to the Blessed Sacrament

There are many devotions practiced in the Catholic Church. Some are practiced in all countries of the world and by persons

---

*This prophetic statement comes from the Encyclopedia Brittanica-showing how widespread such concerns were just a generation ago (1955).

of every age, station and walk of life. The most universally practiced devotion is devotion to the Blessed Sacrament. It is the focal point of all devotions and life in the church. All other devotions group themselves around it as an appendage, for the others celebrate the mysteries of our Faith, but this is God Himself. It is the devotion of all races, of all lands, of all ages, of all classes, of all times.

No devotion can compare in dignity, holiness and power with our Lord Jesus Christ present in the Blessed Sacrament. In other devotions we honor God's creatures, but in the Blessed Sacrament we honor the Creator Himself.

The Hope and Salvation of the World

The supreme teachers, the Popes, have been unanimous in proclaiming that the Holy Eucharist is the hope and salvation of the world in our evil and dangerous era. They have endeavored, by word and example, to bring the faithful more closely to Jesus Christ in the Holy Eucharist that they may draw from Him the light and strength needed in overcoming their temptations, anxieties and difficulties.

Pope Leo XIII said:

> Our Lord came to the aid of each great tribulation with a special devotion. The present and future tribulations of the Church and of nations are greater than at any other period, and their per-

secution is more dangerous than those of previous times. Hence, the devotion which God sends to the succor of His Church and of the nations at the present time is the devotion to the Most Holy Eucharist. It is the highest of all devotions. Preach this ever and always. Holy Communion must again be received frequently, yes, daily; the practices of the first Christian centuries must again be adopted.

Christ on Earth

The astronauts' walking on the moon is hailed around the world as the most incredible feat and the greatest achievement ever of man's ingenuity. One of the more profound statements, however, was: "The miracle is not that man walked on the moon, but that the Son of God walked on the earth!"

Man ascended in pride; Christ descended in humility. Man overcame the gravity of earth; Christ the gravity of sin. Man searched for stones; Christ for souls. Man sought his origin; Christ his end. A flapping flag tells man was there; a flickering light—Christ is here!

Appendix
Special Citations and Prayers

Father Faber's Comments on the Eucharist*

One moment, and there is bread in the priest's hands, and wine in the chalice...it would be the grossest of idolatries to offer any manner of worship to that senseless substance. One moment, and the Body of our Lord is at the Right Hand of the Father, receiving in the splendor of its ravishing magnificence the worship of the prostrate hierarchies of heaven.

Another moment, and what was bread is God. A word was whispered by a creature, and lo! he has fallen down to worship, for in his hands is his Creator, produced there by

---

*Fr. Frederick Faber, *The Blessed Sacrament*

his own whispered word. One moment and at the bidding of a trembling, frightened man, Omnipotence has run through a course of resplendent miracles, each more marvellous than a world's creation out of nothing, not as swiftly as a well-skilled finger sweeps down the keys of an instrument, but unspeakably more swiftly; for here there has been no succession: in one and the same moment the whole range of these miracles was traversed and fulfilled.

There is the selfsame Body which the Holy Ghost fashioned out of Mary's blood. There is the self-same Soul that sprung in the fullness of its beauty from the sea of nothingness. There is the self-same Person of the Eternal Word who in Mary's womb assumed that Body and that Soul to Himself. Only in this is the altar more wonderful than the room at Nazareth, that here many times a day, and on tens of thousands of other altars, from the northern fringes of everlasting snow to where the exuberant foliage of the tropics droops into the warm seas, and simultaneously on thousands of altars at once, this stupendous mystery is accomplished; and through the instrumentality, not of a sinless mother, but of unworthy, faulty priests.

Moreover a new code of existence, without local extension, is conferred upon the Body of Christ, in addition to the mode which it already possessed in heaven. And the sun shines in at the Church windows, and the tapers burn unconsciously on the altar, and the flowers shed their fragrance from the vases, while the great mystery is being enacted.

But though inanimate nature has not wherewith to suspect it, and though the senses are deceived and penetrate not beyond the sacramental veils, the very miracle of whose continued existence they are unable to report, the mystery is no secret; the bended knee, the bowed head, the beaten breast, the shrouded face, the instantaneous hush, has revealed that there is not a Catholic child in the Church who does not know, and love, and fear, and worship with his heart's heart the transcending mystery of love.

Msgr. Vaughn's Analogy*

Suppose that some unknown person were to come from another world, and producing a small vessel should say: "Here is a small oval receptacle made out of lime, and filled with a thick glutinous substance. Keep it carefully for a few weeks in a warm and even temperature, and it will gradually transform itself into a

*Msgr. John S. Vaughn, *Thoughts for All Times.*

superb watch." One would instinctively exclaim, "Nonsense!" "How foolish; impossible!"

Yet, strange as it may seem, what happens continually in nature is analogous to what I have proposed, only immeasurably more mysterious.

A watch is a beautiful, complicated thing of many parts admirably put together and most cunningly devised. But a bird is immeasurably more beautiful, more complicated, and a creature of a far greater number of most elaborate parts, far more exquisitely put together. Take the egg of any bird you please, let us say a goldfinch. When first laid by the hen, what is it but an oval receptacle of lime filled with a thick glutinous substance? This substance is structureless and shapeless, and for the most part, almost colorless; yet, keep it in a suitable temperature for a few weeks and it will become gradually transformed by the power of God acting through natural laws; not into a watch, but into what is infinitely more admirable, into a living, breathing, sentient bird.

Within the fragile shell, no thicker than your nail, changes and transformations are being gradually made, so singular and mysterious, that I know not to what I can compare them, unless it be to the changes that the earth went through during the six days of creation, when God brooded over the face of the deep, and drew order and symmetry out of chaos. A living being is being formed. The bones of leg and wing, the spinal column with all its articulations, the skull and pointed beak and sharp claws emerge, as if by magic, from out of the liquid mass.

Not only is each brittle bone beautifully fashioned, exquisitely finished, and polished as smooth as ivory—each different, yet all correlated—but they are knit together and adjusted with the utmost precision and harmony, and built up, without hands, according to a distinct and definite plan. Flesh and skin envelop the entire skeleton; while throughout the whole there run innumerable channels and secret passages and ducts carrying arterial and venous blood from one extremity to the other. Invisible fingers are still molding the beautiful form of the bird, and arranging its interior organs of nutrition and digestion, and forming that marvelous heart on the strictest scientific principles, which is to keep forcing the blood circulating through the whole organism.

Still the work proceeds. The original glutinous liquid is all that the shell contains, or has ever contained. From it, therefore, and from nothing else, is drawn the gorgeous plumage that is to be the glory of the bird. The wings are supplied with long, light, pointed feathers, suitable for flight, and the breast is coated with softest down of many brilliant colors. All is daintily finished, delicately tinted, and Divinely made. Yet, notice. The fragile shell is till intact. No fresh material has been introduced. All—bones, muscles, veins, blood, brain, skull, beak, claws, feathers, liver, heart, lungs, etc.,—have been constructed out of the same simple structureless liquid protoplasm.

Matter enough, but no more than enough, has been stored within the shell for the construction of every limb, muscle and organ, and all else down to the smallest fragment of down that goes to complete the perfection of the bird. At last the shell breaks. The fluid has disappeared, and in its place a bird darts forth instinct with life; with glancing eyes, and flapping wings, and palpitating heart, and with a throat eloquent with song and softly warbled harmonies.

What a stupendous miracle of Divine power and wisdom!

Saint John Bosco's Famous Vision

Devout Catholics have often heard of the famous vision of St. John Bosco. The great Marian Saint and patron of youth looked ahead to this century. In this most striking vision the Church was seen in the form of the Barque of Peter and was in great jeopardy. A great storm had risen at sea and the Mighty Ship of the Church was being violently tossed about in the mighty wind and waves, so much so that is almost seemed as though it could sink. At the helm was the Pope steering the ship safely to port and to calmness through two pillars that rose from the waters into the sky.

On one pillar was the Holy Eucharist and beneath was the inscription "Salvation of Believers." On the other pillar was a statue of the Immaculate Virgin Mary, at her feet the inscription "Help of Christians." By steering the ship between the two pillars and mooring the Barque of Peter to them, the Church was guided to safety.

When You Miss Holy Communion

You miss a personal visit with Jesus. You lose a special increase of sanctifying grace. You lose a quota of sacramental graces. You lose the opportunity of having all of your venial sins wiped away. You miss the opportunity of having remitted a part, or all, of your temporal punishment due to your sins. You lose the spiritual joy that comes from a fervent Holy Communion. You lose part of the glory your body would enjoy at its resurrection on the last day. You lose the greater degree of glory you would possess in heaven for all eternity.

Anima Christi

Soul of Christ, sanctify me.
Body of Christ, save me.
Blood of Christ, inebriate me.
Water from the side of Christ, wash me.
Passion of Christ, strengthen me.
O good Jesus, hear me.
Within Thy wounds, hide me.
Suffer me not to be separated from Thee.
From the malicious enemy, defend me.
In the hour of my death, call me.
And bid me come to Thee.
That with Thy saints, I may praise Thee,
For ever and ever. Amen.

Prayer before Communion*

Come my Lord, implant Yourself in my heart. Lock its doors forever. I want nothing cheap to enter it and take away the love that belongs to You. You alone must run my life. If I swerve from You, steer me straight once more. Make me search for one pleasure: the pleasure of pleasing You. Make me yearn

*By St. Alphonsus Liguori.

for one joy: the joy of visiting You. Make me crave for one delight: the delight of receiving Your body. So many people chase after such hollow things! But all I care about is Your love, and I am here to beg it from You today. Let me forget myself and keep You ever before my mind. Amen.

Prayer after Communion*

Dear Jesus, accept this Holy Communion as my Viaticum, as if I were on this day to die. Grant that Thy most adorable Body and Blood may be the last remembrance of my soul; the sacred names of Jesus, Mary and Joseph my last words; my last affection an act of the purest, the most ardent love of Thee, and a sincere sorrow for my sins; my last consideration to expire in Thy divine arms adorned with the gifts of Thy holy grace. Amen.

Chaplet of Divine Mercy

While the Polish nun, Sister Faustina Kowalska, was praying before the Blessed Sacrament, our Lord revealed Himself to

*This prayer originated in Ireland.

her! There were pink and white rays of Divine light emanating from His Sacred Heart, radiating throughout the entire chapel. Whenever someone came into the chapel for a visit, these divine rays would go forth from Jesus and encircle the whole world. Jesus explained that each person coming before Him in the Blessed Sacrament represented all humanity and that every man, woman and child on the face of the earth experiences a new effect of His goodness, grace, love and mercy for each holy hour made in His divine Presence. Jesus gave Sister Faustina the following prayer to be said by those who go before Him in the Blessed Sacrament to appeal for His divine mercy on all mankind—it can be prayed on the beads of the Rosary:

"First say one Our Father, Hail Mary, and I Believe. [Apostle's Creed]. Then on the large beads say the following words: 'Eternal Father, I offer You the Body and Blood, Soul and Divinity of Your dearly beloved Son, Our Lord Jesus Christ, in atonement for our sins and those of the whole world.'"

"On the smaller beads say the following words: 'For the sake of His sorrowful Passion, have mercy on us and on the whole world."

In conclusion you are to say these words three times: "Holy God, Holy Mighty One, Holy Immortal One, have mercy on us and on the whole world."

Bibliography

Bernier, Paul J., *S.S.S., Bread From Heaven*, Paulist Press, N.Y. 1977.

Bonniwell, William, O.P., *Life of Blessed Margaret of Castello*, Tan Books and Publishers, Rockford, Ill., 1979.

Butler, Alban; Thurston, Herbert, S.J.: Attwater, Donald, *The Lives of the Saints,* 12 volumes, P.J. Kenedy and Sons, N.Y. 1936.

Catoir, John, *Christopher News Notes,* N.Y.

Colledge, Edmund, O.S.A., Walsh, James, S.J., *Following the Saints*, Good Will Publishers, Inc., Gastonia, N.C., 1972.

Cruz, Joan Carroll, *Eucharistic Miracles*, Tan Books and Publishers, Rockford, Ill., 1987.

Dalgairns, John, *The Holy Communion*, Duffy and Co., Dublin, Ireland, 1892.

Davis, John F., Msgr., *An Audience with Jesus*, Daughters of St. Paul, Boston, Ma., 1973.

Dubay, Thomas, S.M., *Fire Within*, Ignatius Press, San Francisco, Ca., 1989.

Dittami, Mario L., O. Carm., *Family Lives of the Saints*, Volume II, Carmelite Missions, Darien, Ill., 1981.

Duffy, Regis, O.F.M., *Real Presence,* Harper and Row Publishers, San Francisco, Ca., 1982.

Escriva, Josemaria, Msgr., *The Way,* Scepter Publishers, New Rochelle, N.Y., 1985.

Etlin, Lukas, O.S.B., *Eucharistic Miracles,* Benedictine Convent of Perpetual Adoration, Clyde, Mo., 1952.

Evely, Louis, *We Are All Brothers*, Herder and Herder, N.Y., 1966.

Eymard, St. Peter Julian, 9 books: *The Real Presence, Holy Communion, Eucharistic Retreats, The Eucharist and Christian Perfection I, The*

Eucharist and Christian Perfection II, A Eucharistic Hand Book, Our Lady of the Blessed Sacrament, Month of St. Joseph, In the Light of the Monstrance, Emmanuel Publications, Cleveland, Ohio, 1980.

Faber, Frederick, D.D., *The Blessed Sacrament*, Tan Books and Publishers, Rockford, Ill., 1978.

Fagan, Sean, *Sacraments, the Gestures of Christ,* edited by Denis O'Callaghan, Sheed and Ward, N.Y., 1964.

Grace, William J., S.J., *Catholic Quote* (mag.), Valparaiso, Nebraska.

Guzie, Tad, S.J., *Jesus in the Eucharist*, Paulist Press, N.Y., 1974.

Hamrogue, John M., C.S.S.A., *Five Steps to Greater Holiness*, Liguori Publications, Liguori, Mo., 1988.

Herbst, Winfrid, S.D.S., *Eucharistic Whisperings,* Volumes: 2,4,5,8, The Salvatorian Fathers, St. Nazianz, Wisc., 1926.

Hoever, Hugo, S.O. Cist., Ph.D., *Lives of the Saints*, Catholic Book Publishing Co., N.Y., 1977.

Huget, Pere, *Consoling Thoughts of St. Francis de Sales*, Frederick Dustet Co., Inc., N.Y., 1910.

Kaczmarek, Louis, *The Wonders She Performs,* Trinity Communications, Manassas, Va., 1986.

Kempf, Constantine, S.J., *The Holiness of the Church in the Nineteenth Century*, Benziger Bros., N.Y., 1916.

Kennedy, Eugene, *A Time For Being Human,* The Thomas More Press, Chicago, Ill., 1977.

Leonard, St., *The Hidden Treasure*, Tan Books and Publishers, Rockford, Ill., 1952.

Liguori, St. Alphonsus de., *The Holy Eucharist,* Redemptorist Fathers, Brooklyn, N.Y., 1934.

Louis of Grenada, O.P., *The Sinners Guide,* Tan Books and Publishers, Inc., Rockford, Ill.

Lorit, Sergius, C., Charles de Foucald, *The Silent Witness*, New City Press, N.Y., 1966.

Marcetteau, B.F., S.S., *Come Follow Me,* Volume II, The Bruce Publishing Co., Milwaukee, Wisc., 1947.

Marmion, Dom Columba, O.S.B., *Christ In His Myseries,* B. Herber Book Co., St. Louis, Mo., 1924.

Merton, Thomas, *Life of Holiness*, Doubleday Image Books, Garden City, N.Y., 1962.

Moran, Patrick R., *Day by Day with the Saints*, Our Sunday Visitor Inc., Huntington, In., 1985.

Muller, Michael, C.S.S.R., *The Blessed Eucharist, Our Greatest Treasure,* Tan Books and Publishers, Inc., Rockford, Ill., 1973.

Nichol, Donald, *Holiness*, The Seabury Press, N.Y., N.Y., 1981.

O'Brien, John A., *The Faith of Millions*, Our Sunday Visitor, Huntington, In., 1974.

Poage, Godfrey, C.P., *In Garments All Red*, Ave Maria Institute, Washington, N.J., 1950.

Pohle, Joseph, Rt. Rev. Msgr., Ph.D., D.D., *The Sacraments,* Volume II, B. Herder Book Co., London, England, 1917.

Powers, Joseph M., S.J., *Eucharistic Theology*, Herder and Herder, N.Y., 1967.

Quinlan, Francis, C.S.C., *Five Steps to Holiness*, Liguori Publications, Liguori, Mo., 1989.

Royer, Franchon, *The Life of St. Anthony Mary Claret*, Tan Books and Publishers, Rockford, Ill., 1957.

Rumble, Leslie, M.S.C.; Carty, Mortimer, *Radio Replies*, 3 volumes, Tan Books and Publishers, Inc., Rockford, Ill., 1979

Segur, Msgr., de, *Holy Communion,* The Paulist Press, N.Y., 1915.

Sheehan, M., Most Rev., D.D., *Apologetics and Catholic Doctrine*, M.H. Gill and Son, Ltd., Dublin, Ireland, 1929.

Sheppard, Lancelot C., *Don Bosco*, The Newman Press, Westminster, Md., 1957.

Schouppe, F.X., S.J., *Hell*, Tan Books and Publishers, Inc., Rockford, Ill.

Stevens, Clifford, *The One Year Book of Saints,* Our Sunday Visitor, Inc., Huntington, Ind., 1989.

Tonne, Arthur, Msgr., *Stories for Sermons*, Vol. 10, St. John Church-Pilsen, Marion, Kansas, 1958.

Van Acken, Bernard, S.J., *The Holy Eucharist*, The Newman Press, Westminster, Md., 1958.

Vaughn, John S., Msgr., *Thoughts For All Times*, St. Vincent's Mission House, Springfield, Ma., 1910.

Vianney, St. John, compiled and arranged by W.M.B., *Thoughts of the Cure D'Ars,* Templegate, Ill., 1967.

Zimmer, Luke, SS.CC., *Apostolic Renewal*, Christ the King Center, Pomona, Ca., 1973.

Index of Saints and Blesseds Cited in the Text